REVIEWS FROM THE FIRST EDITION

Self-help in the real sense after so long

Beautiful book. It's a book with energy that guides you into the most profound messages in the book. I love self-help books, but after reading this one, I feel all of them take you into a loop giving the same message. This book here has a different message on every page. The author, Sahar, seems to be someone who has selflessly shared all that we can handle. Loved it. After Wayne Dyer, someone who will fill his vacuum. *Twice Born* is a blessing for many.

—Ranji Pannu
Reviewed in India on 7 October 2019

My bible for life! Easy to read with so much depth! May we all be twice-born after reading it.

I started reading *Twice Born* a month ago. It has now become my bible. I read and re-read pages I've marked every day... it's so deep and intense, and I can so well relate to it. I want to thank Sahar for writing this beautiful book to guide so many of us looking for answers. Her knowledge and knowing are astounding, and penning it down for us to understand the workings of the universe is something else. Thank you, Sahar, so looking forward to your 2nd book!

Love and light,
—Smita Dhar
Reviewed in India on 17 November 2019

A must read for growth (spiritual and personal)

This book will shake you awake from your slumber. When you feel deadlocked or feel that your life is moving in a loop. Even after doing different kinds of practices and meditations, you feel not reaching where you would want to in your personal growth; then this book is a must-read. Initially, I didn't understand what the author was trying to say, but I allowed myself to unlearn and read it like a blank slate... I found the message that has changed me on a deeper level. After (reading) this book, I have changed on a profound level for the better. Every time I read it, the book gives more messages to apply and grow. It's not just any self-help book; it's going to change your life fundamentally. A must-read for spiritual growth, break deadlocks and patterns, reach your higher potential, and see life from a different perspective. Brilliantly written. Thanks to the author for sharing her journey in such a heart-to-heart kind of manner

—Anonymous Amazon Customer
Reviewed in India on 25 January 2020

Just an amazing and an eye-opening book.

It's a very beautifully written book which explains so many complicated topics in a very simple and lucid way. Every line has depth in it. By writing her own story in the book, the author also inspires us. I have read this book twice. This book is like a bible to me. With any question in mind, you read the topic concerned, and you will surely find your answer. A must-read for all the seekers!

—Shiba Mittal
Reviewed in India on 7 March 2020

A Must Read...

This book is a must-read for all; this is by far the most simple, honest & wonderful book I've read. Written by charming transformational life coach, Sahar Gharachorlou, the book unfolds many mysteries of life, answer questions & queries of life with her real-life references & experiences in a simple & interesting manner. It will remain a guiding light for me. I congratulate & thank Sahar, the author, for thinking of sharing such a wonderful life experience with the world. This is definitely going to make a difference in the lives of readers.

—Kamal Preet
Reviewed in India on 20 September 2020

Exceptional and a must-buy guide for life.
According to science, energy is constant. It can neither be created nor destroyed. It just changes form. Accordingly, the human soul, too, is an energy form that must be changing forms in each life. I lived by this concept, but this book has doubly reinforced my faith. Currently reading it the second time, and I am sure it will be my goto guide for the rest of my life. Thank you, Sahar, for creating such a gem and giving my staggered beliefs a concrete form.

—Dr Ankur Dixit
Reviewed in India on 10 April 2020

The book makes you happy and light
All good books are simple :) That's what makes *Twice Born* a must-read! I loved the simplicity with which the author Sahar Gharachorlou drives home the message. It's not a preachy kind of regular self-help book; it's like a humorous and light homecoming book. I truly loved the book and Sahar's story-telling!

—Dr Anu
Reviewed in India on 10 November 2019

Heart opener!
To be honest, I was never inclined to read books on spiritual/life coach genres. Finally succumbed to my wife's pressure, and I am so glad I did. A very intriguing book, (it) helps you to see through beyond conceptualized

thoughts. It has helped me break many patterns and made me understand life as it is supposed to happen to us. Thank you, Sahar. (We are) Waiting for your second book.

—Jatin H.
Reviewed in India on 21 March 2020

(The) Soul is the essence
It's an amazing conversation (wrong to call it a book) because Sahar very aptly puts words and sentences in such a way as if she is talking to the author. A must-read for everyone, every page has a profound answer to thoughts that keep popping up in our head about who we are and where we are going. Thank you for this effort

—Anonymous Amazon Customer
Reviewed in India on 23 February 2020

Reading this Book was an amazing journey!
Thank you so much, Sahar Gharachorlou, for writing this wonderful book. All the spiritual concepts are well-explained, and all your amazing experiences are helping the reader connect with you! Thank you once again! Must-read book!

—Anonymous Amazon Customer
Reviewed in India on 8 July 2020

This Book Heals Your Soul
First Review:
I'm going to give my full review after I've read the full book, but I couldn't stop myself from sharing that moment I got on to Chapter-1, P-1, I read it once and reread it and OMG.. so totally related to the words that are almost like a portal that is about to open to what you need to know. I wanted to deposit the words in my savings accounts of words wisdom.

The book was a gift from a dear friend a couple of months ago, but I got my hands on it now as I gave it to my Dad to read it first. He's an ex-army man who has also written novels and poetry books on Indian soldiers. He's read many books in his life, but this he kept rereading. I couldn't get my hands on the book because he read TWICE first and then would keep rereading, opening a random chapter or a page, and would share his thoughts on the LIFE LIVED of the TWICE BORN and how simple yet grippingly she has explained everything. My Dad calls it the BEST BOOK EVER! More power to you, Sahar.

Second Review

This Book HEALS YOUR SOUL and gives ULTIMATE JOY. The power of expression and the spellbinding words speak to your soul. I so wish that the book never finished. It was like a lifeline to my anxiety & depression and not being able to find my path or purpose, in total desolation and losing hope. While reading this book, I got so many answers to the unasked questions too. I'd sleep & wake up with this book next to me, and with every read, I felt that Sahar, the healing soul, the *Twice Born*, was with me every step of the way. I felt connected to her, and that was very comforting. The book feels like a personal tête à tête and a healing session. It's amazing how someone who has gone through so much fire and life tests smiles like an angel giving love & healing just with her virtual presence. I've read many books on similar topics. This one is an amalgamation of all those, simply put, and opens portals in your mind and expands your limited thinking to limitless perspective. I'm spoiled after reading this book. The soul seeks more; the mind wants more, the heart awaits.

Love, Light & Angel Blessings
—Monicaa
Reviewed in India on 30 May 2020

One solution to every Problem — *Twice Born* **(I take it everywhere I go)**
'Twice Born' — a wonderful guide that helps us find all solutions to our doubts, confusion, and problems. It helped me to understand and accept that 'I am the only in charge of my life' and 'How can I use this power for everything and anything.' I am one of those fortunate ones who could meet Sahar (through her 'magical' workshops) before she shared her guidance in the form of a priceless gift — *Twice Born*, so when I was reading this book, I could feel that she is talking to me one-to-one which helped me to connect more.

It comprises everything that one needs. Now, when I feel like seeking help, or get low in life, or need clarity on something which is bothering me, all I do is open this friend-like book and read it. It provides me what I am exactly looking for. This book works! I take it everywhere I go.

I want to write about how every chapter of this masterpiece fixes every aspect of one's life, but then I realize that there is no fun in it. So go and get it for yourself. Lastly, one of Sahar's teaching says that replacing 'should', 'must', 'have to' words with 'can' will shift the most of the energy in your lives. So better to avoid such words (Words we speak, listen, READ are really powerful). But here I cannot stop myself by writing — TWICE BORN IS MUST-READ. (I am feeling so grateful and happy that I have this book with me during this period of realization - Quarantine 😊 😷)

—Rajwant
Reviewed in India on 2 May 2020

Doesn't want to Take Charge of Your Life, but encourages 'You' to do it yourself!
Not very often comes a self-help book where the author doesn't want to control your mind and doesn't want you to subscribe to only 'their' method to reach nirvana! *Twice Born* by Sahar is one such book. It doesn't pretend to know all and teach all. On the contrary, it acts like a match to light up your thought process, exhorting you to take control of your life, make your

blueprint, to reach your salvation. Through personal stories honestly stating her good and bad decisions that charted her life course, Sahar acts like an ideal friend who, after gaining insights into the tricks of keeping your life sane, now wants to help her friends to kickstart their journey.

I was initially a little skeptical about the premise. Being an agnostic, talking about 'past-life' regression, etc. made me look at this manuscript as one I couldn't identify with. However, as I read along, I realized that these beliefs, like many others, are just a medium to simplify your journey of discovery of your soul. Whether you approach it from the religious, agnostic, or spiritual direction, if your quest is honest and your intentions clean, all these roads lead to 'personal awareness' which is a pre-requisite for 'personal development'!

—Param Kharbanda
Reviewed in India on 5 December 2019

TWICE BORN is an Eye-Opener ...

The book is an eye-opener. A book that you would want to keep re-reading. So much to contemplate. It's a must book for everyone to have, a book with answers to so many questions that have been lingering deep in us. Doubts, myths, judgments, man-made rules—all these that have been creating fear in our minds. This book is going to clear all the misunderstandings and misconceptions and clear all our doubts. I thank the author, Sahar, for this book is the window for complete awareness. I strongly recommend everyone to read the book.

—Dimple Haresh Mirpuri
Reviewed in India on 28 November 2019

TWICE BORN

Finding Myself, Guiding Others

Sahar Gharachorlou

www.thebrowser.org

Publishers & Booksellers

ISBN – 978-93-88150-12-5
Edition – First

Published in India by –
J.G.S. Enterprises Pvt Ltd
Imprint: The Browser

Publisher's Address –
SCO 14-15, Sector 8-C, Chandigarh 160 009
Email – service@thebrowser.org
Website – www.thebrowser.org
Copyright © 2020 Sahar Gharachorlou
All rights reserved

Printed in India
Cover design, typesetting & layout by 99beagles

THE BR●WSER
www.thebrowser.org
Publishers & Booksellers

For my beloved father, who believed in
me more than anyone else.
To ease his pain, the pain no one saw,
because I see clearly now.

Who am I?
I am no one and yet everyone.
I am the very dance of existence.
I am the dance, the music and the dancer.
I am the very ocean of existence, gushing
through me wave by wave, drop by drop.
I am the play, the actor, and the stage.
I am 'The Dream' and 'The Dreamer.'
In you, I am the reflection I deny.
In you, I am the hope I so repulse.
It's not you or me that I rebuff.
It's not the dream that I deny.
It's not the dance, the music, the play,
the stage, the wave, the ocean that I debunk.
In you & me, it's the dreamer that I deny.

CONTENTS

PREFACE TO THE SECOND EDITION

When you do things from your soul, you feel a river moving in you, a Joy.
—Rumi

When I first started to pen down *Twice Born* in 2018, I wasn't sure why I was writing it. I just knew my soul had an urge; it wanted to say and to be heard. I didn't quite know what it was that it had to talk about, I just had a sense of urgency, as if I was running out of time and as if those waiting to hear what my soul had to say shouldn't be delayed any further.

When the force became too strong, and I could no more hold my soul's calling captive, everything flew through me, a force beyond my control was in-charge, and this book gushed out in just 42 days. I am so glad I answered that call, and I urge my readers to follow suit because that's when the river of joy starts moving in you.

The overwhelming response I have gotten from my readers is the reward of me facing my fears and letting *Twice Born* take birth through me.

I thank all my readers, students and clients for their love and support, and hope that the additions made to this book will be of value.

This book is a compilation of my real-life story, messages from the masters and other realms, and case studies of my clients. As you read along, you may find it a strange story, shaping up in unusual ways.

As a metaphysical therapist, I always look for the root cause of a challenge in the realm of the spirit and heal the issue from the soul to heal the mind and body. Interestingly, the metaphysical cause of any virus (with some variation as to which organ the virus affects the most) is the need for un-conditionality. As I was editing my book, I wondered – have we come to a space of chaos as a result of judgement about ourselves and our environment, to the extent that we can no more breathe freely. Are these times telling us that we have been separated and disconnected from love long enough for our lungs not to be able to take the discrimination that's in the air anymore?

Is it time for us to awaken to what we have created? Do we have so much fear within that it had to manifest and scare the whole world? This book is about allowing you to choose. Maybe this is the time you wish to choose a new reality for yourself and the generations to come. Perhaps it is time we realize that life is larger than our fears and the only way forward is to move together, in love and faith.

My prayer is that this book facilitates you to find the love within, and spread it fearlessly so that your soul too, awakens to the river of joy inside, and may you allow it to flow through you.

Love.

PREFACE TO THE FIRST EDITION

A combination of real-life stories; of my clients as well as mine, their case studies, some messages from the realm of the 'spirit', loads of research and observations that transformed the way people live, helped me bring this book to life. This book is a sincere attempt to present deeper wisdom, without which our life journey becomes just hit and trial. Without understanding the essence of the universe and ways of 'The Source', it is impossible to move in the right direction. Without clarity, we continue to move in circles. I feel humbled and blessed for being able to present this work, where I share my world view. It has been an extremely fulfilling journey with highs and lows; brimming with ecstasy, plummeting to the pits and yet holding on to life's essence through exhilarating ways.

Through this book, I wish to remind that you are the highest form of evolution on this beautiful planet called Earth and yet the most spoilt child of this universe. Ignorance is the single biggest cause of man's misery. Of its Creator, we have remained mostly ignorant. Our gift of evolutionary choices remains unwrapped by many. We have been misguided by a selected few, who controlled us simply because we didn't know who we truly were. The beast of power has proved to be the most demonic enemy to the beauty of the human soul. This book is a soul to soul, heart to heart exchange of that which we all have, 'the knowing.' A touch of what I have witnessed over the past thirteen years while working with people from all walks of life – doling out truths that are so simple, yet profound. Powerful enough to free us from the slavery of myths, religions and dogmas created by those in a position of power, including the self-proclaimed 'gurus.'

It is a negligible yet sincere effort to offer you the wisdom that has opened my eyes, warmed my heart and charged my soul. I hope that what changed my life and made me move from a dimension of pain and disbelief to a state of joy and bliss, would ignite the same spark in you too. I have tried to dish out a fraction of what I have witnessed in a simple and easy language. I pray that I can be a channel of divine guidance to help you get in touch with the depth of your soul, the unique expression with which you have come so that when you leave, you have left behind your signature for the world to cherish.

I may sound a bit harsh and on the face sometimes, but I want you to bear with me and focus on the message. The real 'me' is brutally honest and upfront, refusing to glorify or demean anything. I see black as black and white as white, simply because there are no shades of grey in this universe. I thank you in anticipation for hearing me as I express my truth. This book is written from a space of love and observation. It is about being who I am, letting everyone be who they are and yet choosing 'grace' above all.

We human beings glorify certain aspects of life, the parts that boost our egos – such as close relationships, social status, our forefather's beliefs and way of life, and even children's achievements – simply because the ego demands it. It is, by far, the worst thing we have done to human consciousness. In this book, I talk about everyone as I see them. It is the perspective of a free soul with a unique journey, sharing with you what showed up on her path. And it is in no way to dishonour anyone's belief, sentiments or culture. I wish you see it in the same light as I do.

Today, I truly believe that nothing can ever go wrong; no one is ever wrong. Everything that has ever happened, is happening or will happen in the future, no matter how ugly and painful it may feel or look, is always the best for all involved – in terms of evolution and growth. I have no intention of proving any individual, community, cult, culture or religion wrong. I aim to present another way of seeing and perceiving life, which has not only changed and transformed my life but also the lives of many more who chose to see it differently.

Let's understand that pain is inevitable, but suffering is a choice each one of us is making every moment with every decision we make. I also believe that absolutely everything in life is subject to change. And 'change' we must.

I wish to introduce to you a simple way of being; one that has freed me and so many from what we perceive as a complex phenomenon – 'life'; because simplicity and ease is the design of existence, joy is our essence. It is only through freedom that joy can be experienced. Freedom from all the lies we have ever told ourselves, the myths we have believed in, the emotions with which we have lived; freedom from past glories and miseries. I desire to transform the glorified spiritual concepts to approachable, understandable and doable practices so that they become your way of life.

My deepest gratitude to all my friends, some of whom I refer to as earth 'angels' in this book and in my life. (I have truly been blessed with a handful of them.) I thank my angels Sanjiv B, Smriti Singh, Namrata Singh, Jaspreet Chawla and Angelina, my family which motivated me to start this quest, my book coach Esther Molenar, and my friend Ira who was the first person to plant the seed of writing a book in my head. I am thankful to my teachers, both in the physical form and from the 'spirit realm,' and most importantly, to this existence and Mother Earth, this most beautiful school of life. I also owe it to all my clients and students for being the channel of learning and growth in the most profound and magical way I could have ever asked for. Heartfelt thanks to Vikrant Parmar and Sheela Roy, my editors for their help in shaping this book. I am particularly grateful to Sheela Roy, who encouraged me every time I hit the writer's block, and whose belief in my message made me complete this book. Last but not least, cheers to my soul, which has chosen to express itself through this book.

Book One
The Calling

1

When the Soul Chose to Fight

Often, a major life-altering painful experience brings about a turning point in a person's life. Then, one consciously chooses the path of spiritual growth and self-realisation, usually referred to as—'The Calling.'

We human beings are the most audacious, least grateful species ever to wonder if there can be anything beyond our over-inflated egos and limited intellect. Hence, we all need a wake-up call, sooner than later. The calling, as they say, is usually a painful incident; one that brings us to the point of misery and unending questions like 'why me?' It can be a mishap, the loss of a loved one, or a major accident, chronic disease or any form of extreme, debilitating experience.

The universe certainly has no personal enmity with us; it is our ignorance and lack of awareness that causes the universe to eventually punch us in the face after many soft and subtle wake-up whispers. The universe, like any loving mother, would have tried to wake the spoilt child that we are from the featherbed of ignorance with kisses on the forehead, followed by gentle nudges. But we are so deeply asleep that we don't realise we are getting delayed for the school of life. We continue to be deep in slumber until the day when there can be no further delay. We would not only miss the bus but also cause harm to all others. At this point, the universe decides to either punch us in the face, or throw a bucket of icy cold water on our heads, and shock us into facing our truth.

In my case, my dumbness was way too overpowering over my shamelessness. My calling happened with a telephone call. It wasn't any normal call; it took the universe to dial my number and that too, twice! Now that I look back at my life, I realise that due to circumstances, my DNA, ancestral imprinting and the family I had chosen, there was no other way for the universe to knock me off my reverie. I had lived way too long and way too strongly in my cocoon, refusing to budge. The nightmare had to end, but sometimes, like patients in the emergency room, we need shock therapy to jolt the entire system. My life had collapsed completely, but I was too numb to know.

The first call was in early November 2009; it was my mother on the other side. She was crying, which was very unlike her; she was in distress, which was so alien to her. In a hush-hush voice, she spoke rather haltingly, "Postpone your plans of visiting home; there seems to be a complaint of you having converted from Islam to Sikhism." For any Muslim, this is a sin and a crime; we have all been told that in any country under Islamic Law, conversion is a punishable offence, and it leads to capital punishment. Till date, I don't know if there was any such complaint, and even if there was, well it could be false, but how could one prove it?

At that moment, my world came crashing down. All that I could relate to and remember was that a couple of months before this, my then husband's friend, Rahul, had visited my office portraying to be my well-wisher. He had said that it would be better for me to leave India because my husband was planning to frame me in a false case by complaining to the Iranian Embassy that I had converted to Sikhism, and as I was no more living with him, they should cancel my visa in India.

I had listened to him, laughed it out and said, "Let him do it—when it happens, I will see." I felt it was just a threat because of his smashed ego. After all, we had separated, and since it was me who had decided to leave, he was bound to be upset. I had rejected his thought process and his family's way of treating me. They say the male ego feels rejection more strongly (undoubtedly a belief originated out of male-dominated societies).

However much I thought about it, I could never believe that someone who claimed to love me and with whom I had shared over 1300 days of my life, 31200 hours to be precise, who claimed to be in love even though I had evidence of him paying for sex in the Mumbai dance bars, would want to harm me in any way. Someone who would leave me for a week and go to his parents' house because his dog was ill, couldn't be so inhuman. It was only later that I realised that he believed that my value was lesser than his dog. Well, better late than never. Now I understand that if you are married to a narcissist, he will use any method to break you down; by abusing you emotionally, mentally, verbally and sometimes even sexually. A narcissist wants to crush your very spirit so that he can feel superior.

I was brought up in an extremely protected environment; born to a wounded, self-absorbed mother. Don't take me wrong, my mother is my best friend and a great woman, but wounded and hurt. (I completely adore her, but I wish to share the truth as it is.) I was so used to that frequency of energy that I could not recognise the animalistic side of human consciousness in my husband at that time. The difference was that my mother had some values; we were taught never to think ill of anyone, never to harm anyone. My father, even though a Muslim, told us about the Zoroastrian teachings of Ahura Mazda, "Think good, Talk good and Act good." He strictly followed these three principles, at least in his speech, but that was good enough for me to imbibe them. My untiring effort was targeted towards winning over my mother's love and attention; to be a good girl. Later, when I became an 'Inner Child' therapist, I realised all my attempts to be 'the good girl' were because I was the forgotten child who was desperately trying to win her mother's affection.

When my mother called me that day and said that there was a complaint, I froze with fear, confusion and disbelief. As I heard her, time stood still. I could not fathom how any human being could be so cruel; it felt like one of those extreme Hollywood movies. Later, I learnt that the soul chooses every minute detail of its plan with such precision that absolutely nothing can be an accident. I had chosen this too, and for a long time, even as a therapist, I have wondered why my soul chose such a messed up plan!

I was still in shock, not knowing that the universe was preparing me for the next blow, the one that would finally push me into becoming who I was supposed to be. The human mind and body are the most beautiful designs in the entire existence; their ability to absorb shock and adjust around its impact is fascinating. It wasn't till I received the second call two weeks later from the foreign registration office in Chandigarh that I realised it was 'my call.'

The memory is so vivid even ten years later. I was sitting in a board meeting for quarterly performance evaluation, engrossed in the presentation of a colleague, mentally preparing for my presentation that was lined up next. I noticed several missed calls from the same number and assuming that they were from a student in panic mode, I decided to take the call before my turn.

It was 'The Call.'

On the other side, I heard a voice saying: "Namaskar! Sahar ji se baat ho sakti hai?" (Namaste! Can I talk to Ms Sahar?)

I don't remember what my reply was, but I could hear, "The Ministry of Home Affairs has cancelled your visa. Please come and collect your exit order, you have 72 hours to leave the country." He muttered a few more words, but all I could hear was my heartbeat, which silenced all else.

I don't even know how I responded, all I could say was, "I am in a board meeting (as if it mattered anymore), give me a day." And, I disconnected the call.

Thanks to my extremely miserable marriage, I had been secretly learning meditation, Reiki and a few other forms of energy healing techniques with which somehow I managed to pull out of my memory. So, I took a few deep breaths, watched myself being washed in pink healing energy and calmed myself down. I checked my hands holding my cellphone to see if they had stopped shaking. I was amazed at how beautifully the techniques had worked. I told myself, "Wow! This stuff works." I checked my eyes in the phone camera, straightened my skirt and marched into the board room and started my presentation. The marvel of the human mind is that it is the most powerful survival mechanism; it will fight tooth and nail to make sure we survive. It even fights itself to make sure we survive, and that is what my mind did at that particular moment. The obedient soldier defended my honour as the only woman in the boardroom; the repercussions were that I was numb for the next eight years of my life. From that moment on, nothing mattered anymore; I became a machine with just one mission—to prove my innocence; to take back my right to live where I wished to. I slowly let go of all those who I knew, numbed my nerves with work and lost sense of time, as also life. I do not have any memory of those eight years, other than my continuous battle to prove myself not guilty.

From what I know of myself then, I cannot imagine how I managed those initial few months. I had powerful execution skills; when it came to the call of duty, commitments and my work, I was a hard taskmaster. I was known to be aggressive, a fighter. I would fight for justice and the sake of others, but deep down I was and still am, a very sensitive, shy and reserved person, so much so that I didn't have it in me to even talk to my ex-husband; he was distant. I was shy in a very non-functional way, so I wrote him a letter to say that I could no more take the humiliation and sarcasm; I wanted myself out of the mess we had created together.

Today, I know the importance of clear communication, and by clear communication, I mean to be able to listen attentively and express appropriately. It is crucial to be able to voice our likes and dislikes in a manner that would help us become more of who we are. The problem arises when we do not honour our truth and that of others; when we judge people as good or bad, right or wrong, adequate or inadequate, when we refuse to see the pain in everyone. The problem arises when we refuse to accept that just like us, everyone is seeking love.

It is interesting how the human mind works. As I kept on working on myself, I learnt that when we go through extreme pain, the soul and the mind choose different mechanisms to survive. The soul decides to either forget or to separate itself from the whole; this is what we call 'soul-loss.' When soul-loss happens, a person genuinely does not remember any painful incident. There is no degree to which a soul can decide not to remember; the capacity of the soul and how much it can take is relative to the level of evolution, gifts, experiences and lessons the soul has chosen to learn. Soul-loss is quite common in case of children who have been subjected to abuse, especially if the perpetrator happens to be a close family member. It can also happen to people who have lost family members in an accident or experienced a sudden shock.

My mind chose to become numb, but fortunately, no soul-loss took place; my soul had chosen to fight. From that point on, my life totally changed. It became more of an adventurous movie and I still wonder how I managed to go through it—maybe I handled it like Scarlett O'Hara in *Gone with the Wind* when she says, "Tomorrow is another day."

A few hours after the phone call had come, when the news had slowly sunk in, I realised I had to inform my office. I talked to my immediate boss, and on seeing his reaction, I realised I didn't have much time. It was Thursday, and I had to leave the country by Sunday. All I could think was that I should handover everything and make sure that no one has to suffer. A typical case of the auto-pilot defence mechanism the mind is so well-equipped with, where I automatically blocked the part of the story that was related to me—it was too painful to deal with it. So I kept busy with something less painful—handing over my work.

It was while explaining to my boss about the situation that I realised I had nowhere to go. My mother had told me that I could not go to Iran, and the authorities had told me that I could not stay in India; it was then I realised that technically I had no place to live in or go to! At that moment of complete helplessness, the universe showed me what I call 'Divine Intervention.' I was shown the way—I met the right person at the right time. I got a chance to present all facts and figures to the authorities concerned, and explain the truth. After going through my file and all other evidence, the Ministry of Home Affairs not only gave me the permit to stay in India but also advised me to change my status in India. It was divine intervention indeed—a series of positive incidents that connect the dots on your path to take you where you need to be for a higher purpose.

It is interesting how every experience, no matter how hard and difficult it might feel at the time, is always happening to help us evolve. Every experience happens because we choose it so. The degree of our struggle is directly proportionate to the size of our ego, our need to hasten our evolution and the love-hate relationship with ourselves.

When I look back today, like anyone else, I laugh at all the hardships I have perceived and been through. I feel I must have been a very stubborn child of life; that, this ever-kind, loving and compassionate universe had to be so harsh to me, to push me hard enough so I could no more escape my path. Too much pain and hardly any answers, that is when we usually ask the golden question, and which is the first door to the awakening of our soul.

It was then that I finally asked, "Why me? What did I do so wrong to deserve this?"

As the legal battle to prove myself innocent in the physical reality began, so began my quest to know 'myself' and where I had gone wrong. My frustration, helplessness and anger at life took me to my first 'Past Life Regression' session. I was born and brought up in Iran; born a Muslim, forbidden to believe in the concept of past life.

However, I was fortunate enough to be born to parents who were open to knowledge and wisdom, and anything that the heart desired. My father was an avid reader and very learned; he was the one who told me to study all religions and choose what my heart believed. My mother believed God was unjust because he gave only suffering to women. It did not matter what they believed, but they helped me open up the ramparts of my mind.

Every soul carefully decides a Soul Plan; it chooses its parents, siblings, and every event and experience, spouse or partner, physical shape, illnesses and almost every single detail that would help it evolve. Our Soul Plan is carved with intrinsic details.

If we can understand the basic laws through which this universe works, it is so much easier to live, to laugh, to be who we are supposed to be. Unfortunately, our conception and how we perceive life is completely fogged by religion as well as religious men. The disease of power and control has seeped into spiritual work as well. We are disillusioned by human-made fears and 'control drama' which only makes us helpless creatures dependent on some holier-than-thou, self-professed, guru or religious men.

I have been fortunate to have some access to these truths, which I would share with you. My only prayer is that you free yourself from untruth and taste the freedom of being your magical self, living a life of abundance as per you; not how someone else has defined magic and abundance. Not even me!

It was six months from the 'Call' that I met an old friend of mine—Mona. We were together in a hostel during our graduation, and I knew her through another friend, but only briefly. We got connected quite accidentally. What I remembered of her was a tomboyish, no-nonsense girl, naughty; the kind that a shy girl like me would stay away from. When we met for coffee after almost twelve years, I was shocked to see the lady in front of me; she was tame, rather sad, and I could not see any trace of her infectious smile with those mischievous shining eyes. Sometimes, shock therapy is most effective; talking to her, I forgot my misery. I couldn't stop myself from comforting her; I knew the only way to understand her pain was to tell her about mine. Well, it worked. We exchanged our stories and decided to be a team, a non-verbal promise; we knew we would be meeting regularly from then on.

Absolutely nothing is accidental; I had to meet Mona as she was my doorway to the world of therapies. It was during one of our English breakfast tea and cheesecake dates that she suggested we should look into the past to understand what karma had led us to this day.

With the background that I came from—a family of absolutely no religious bindings—the word karma sounded Greek to me, but something told me this was the answer. I had to go back to the past to change the present. It is worth mentioning that I am a left-brain person, someone who does not easily believe statements unless backed with solid, black-and-white logic, evidence and results. Yet, I trusted my gut feeling—intuition.

Feelings are the GPS of our soul; if we learn to observe, decode and trust our feelings, we'd never go wrong. Our feelings are the most accurate manifestations of divine guidance; our job is to learn how to trust them and make maximum use of them. For some reason, that is what I did.

There was a time I blamed everyone around me, and more than anyone, God, for how my life had unfolded. I felt life was unfair, asked a thousand times as to why did I have to go through so much. I am sure many of you who are reading this book are either sailing in the same boat or at some point have had similar beliefs.

I grew up in an extremely dysfunctional family; my parents married and divorced each other three times in their life-time. I am not even counting the number of times they stayed separately. As a child, I could never imagine a household where there was no verbal and physical abuse. I blamed my grandparents for having given birth to such children; I blamed my parents for having more than one kid and bringing us to this miserable life where they left us to fend for ourselves. Today, I am certain that no matter what happened and how it happened, it was all a part of my journey; that I had chosen it. Despite all the suffering I experienced, I am certain now that life has always been happening for me and not to me.

Mona was one such miracle; she came to me as divine intervention. Meeting after 12 years, talking about our miserable lives and her efficient skills of locating a therapist, all of which happened within a week of our meeting, was nothing short of a miracle.

We landed up at Dr V's clinic, a filthy, dark, damp and scary place, which looked more like a modern tantric's cave. The so-called clinic was such that neither of us would have dared enter alone. Mona chose to talk first while Dr V kept on taking notes. As Mona continued to speak, I felt the atmosphere getting heavy; there were too many personal questions making Mona uncomfortable. I agreed to go in next even though looking at the filthy place I had no intention of getting therapy done. But as I said, everything is planned: my consultation and meeting with Dr V led me to undergo 598 past life regression sessions till date. (When I originally wrote this book in 2018, I had experienced 527 past lives of mine.) However, Mona never went back after her first session.

This encounter with 'divine intervention' was another one way beyond explanation and comprehension. I have always been intuitive, yet I accredited it to chance. I never took it as a gift like any other person; today I am certain there is absolutely nothing that happens by chance, and that every human being has this gift, just that not everyone is aware of it or knows how to use it. I was a student of psychology; there wasn't much even in those thick books to help me in distress. All the energy healing I had studied was just another attempt of the mind collecting information, but I felt touched by 'The Grace' for the first time during my initial 'Past Life Regression' session.

After that session, everything suddenly started making sense, as if a veil had been lifted; I could see clearly. Those who have experienced the feeling will relate to me when I say the sense of peace, clarity and bliss that prevails as the knots get undone is something to soak in. The richness of the experience is a lasting ecstasy that I still marvel at; to this day, it grows with every new experience. In the past thirteen years, the one thing that has become very evident to me is that 'there is no absolute truth.' The path to self-realisation is to know one's truth, yet some fundamentals shape every perception and are universal. As I learnt more about the universal laws, my search for the truth intensified. This quest shaped my journey as a seeker and a therapist and led me to become a 'seer.' I slowly started to watch the patterns and realised that even though the universe is extremely complex, yet everything happens on auto mode with such precision that if we understand it at a micro-level, we too, would be able to identify complexities with ease. In the upcoming chapters, I will try to decode these concepts, but let me first introduce you to my world—the world of energy and healing.

2

The World of Healing

There are many types of 'energy work': there is light work, and dark work; there is healing work and energy work; there are also therapies.

All of them work with the same thing, the 'energy.' However, depending on the intention and technique used, the intensity, effect and extent of healing would differ. When we do only energy work such as Reiki, Magnified Healing, Pranic Healing etc., what we do is manipulate the energy at the chakra or meridian level without touching its root cause. When we do therapies, we go back and either deal with the metaphysical cause of the disease or we directly go to the belief, the memory that caused the challenge in the body, mind or soul. Therapies such as Hypnosis, Past Life Regression, Inner Child, Shadow Work, Gestalt Therapy etc., help us recognise and address our triggers at any level right from their point of inception. Like anything else, changing the cause would lead to a different effect. To my understanding, a therapist or healer is here to empower those who are looking for guidance.

My desire is for everyone to be empowered to their fullest

potential, where they can lead a joyous life; for that you need to know the way, and that's all you require. Hence, I always tell whoever I meet that anyone who instils any form of fear, dependency and helplessness in them, no matter who he is and how many followers he has, needs to be discarded immediately. This universe is all about love, freedom, growth, harmony and expansion. Anyone operating from fear and control is not real; neither is anyone who follows it.

A light worker would never scare you, nor would he sweet talk you. Calling a spade a spade, recognising the challenge and guiding you to the solution while holding your space with compassion and love, is the approach of a true light worker. His compassion would give you the strength to face your fears and the love would be the driving force, encouraging you to take charge of your life, so that you can find the solution and learn to fight your battles with the belief that you are capable as well as powerful. Anyone who guarantees you a certain result and promises you all the goodies is not being truthful and perhaps, is a conman. No one can guarantee life. Our predestined life is subject to change every ten seconds, how can anyone ever tell you anything with certainty? Neither can anyone other than you change your life for you. When someone tells you about your life, it is because they have worked on the subconscious mind and know how to tap into your energy; they can tell you something about you, which is your reality at that moment. Others may tell you about you, but only you can change your reality. For that having the right guidance is enough, you don't need a saviour. A guide who can show you the way and then let you tread your path is helpful; however, becoming dependent on anyone and thinking they would change your life is very naïve and irresponsible.

Moving on, the difference between spirituality and religion is very distinct. Even though many wish to mix the two, spirituality is about you knowing your self and staying in your own business for your growth. It is the path of sweet trial and sour errors. You practice delving in your truth, which is your soul consciousness, to a level that your mind can no more befool you. It is the ability and strength to see all that is black and white, gorgeous and ugly, about you, as it is, and then having the courage to love, accept and embrace it. Spirituality is a path of self-realisation. You are your own 'Self', your own 'Guru', your own 'Guide', your own 'Master' and even your own 'God.' Spirituality is about seeing the good, the bad and the ugly of yourself, accepting it and loving it, and in doing so, you will be able to do the same with everyone else. There is no judgement, no attachment, only awareness. Your conscience is your case, your court, your jury and your hangman.

Religion, on the other hand, is human-made, it loves poking its nose into everyone's life to the extent of even what they should eat and how they should enter the loo (in certain religions)! It operates from the fear of man and his need for control. It takes away the freedom of choice and with that, the wisdom of knowing. Like 'Chinese Whispers' we truly have no idea if what we believe in and practice is what was handed down to us by the prophets. And even if it was, there is no way we can expect the evolution of consciousness to have come to a standstill and never grown after the dawn of our favourite religion! Hundreds and thousands of years have passed. The nature of this universe demands change and progress, but religion insists you remain stuck and become rigid. Because that is the only way by which you would give your power away. Religions were originally brought forth to help people live with each other in harmony and be more loving. However, like everything else, they fell prey to power-hungry men. I believe they have been distorted beyond repair.

If all religions promote love and brotherhood, then where is it? Why would they condemn each other? How can one God not love the other God? If we have an iota of intelligence, we will refuse any cleric, any church, mosque or temple and absolutely anyone who teaches us how to hate one another and each other's God. Which God would be partial to you because you are a Christian or a Muslim or a Hindu? Which God would disregard another's God? Isn't God all-loving and forgiving?

Religion has become a weapon of mass destruction. It has created fear, which has paralysed 'human consciousness.' Those who have the power to misuse religion have understood the game well and hence, play their cards accurately; they know the only way one can control the wandering mind of man is by either showing him carrots or guns. They use the same old trick to play with your mind; on one side, desire turned to greed, and on the other, fear turned to obsession. And guess what? We have let them play with us forever. The greedy, power-hungry people on top have been ruling us through our fears and desires. They have divided us through borders and nationality, religion and culture, colour and creed so that they can rule our souls and us. Worse is the fact that we happily permit them with our ignorance, not realising the same carrot is being used for all: man's greed and desire for supremacy.

We do have similar species in the spiritual world too, especially manufactured to befool people and rob them of their money and dignity; spiritual leaders who tell you they will take care of your life and get you salvation. I don't blame them for they are here to do business; the only difference is they are selling you your stupidity, and you are gladly buying it. They are telling you how incapable you are of knowing life, and you bow down to them for taking away your power.

Do you know why this is so? Because you are too lazy to take charge, too shameless to be fair; because you are looking for quick-fix solutions. You want to be a gold medallist without having even to practice, forget about the run. You don't wish to pull up your pants, get your hands dirty for your own sake. You have taken the meaning of the word miracle to the extreme of paralysing yourself and well, they love that, because your laziness makes them rich and famous.

The day you realise that this life is your choice and you have planned it, you can change it. When you finally accept you are one hundred per cent responsible for every single act, thought, event, person and situation in your life. You will then have the power to change everything by fixing yourself. That is the day you will be AWAKENED.

And no, that does not mean you will wake up as Buddha the next morning, nor would you become an authority on others lives. Your life will not suddenly become all about roses and blue skies. You won't suddenly wake up one morning finding one billion dollars in your account with your soulmate lying next to you, naked, smelling your favourite scent. Nothing of that sort would happen.

What I mean is you become powerful beyond measure. You taste a sense of freedom that is delicious to your soul and the confidence of knowing you are in charge is enough to conquer any heights. The ride still would be bumpy and rough; this would be the beginning of a mind-blowing adventure called YOU. It won't be easy, but it will be worth it.

When I embarked on this journey, I knew nothing, and maybe that helped. I was a blank slate waiting to be written upon. I discovered as I moved forward and that was my biggest advantage. Sometimes too much information, especially when we cannot discern and differentiate as to what would work for us, makes it more complicated and detrimental to our awakening.

Within a short span of six months after I met Dr V, I was through 19 Past Life Regression sessions. All my holidays and weekends were spent learning new techniques. I learnt over thirteen modalities within that period, and it was interesting that after eight years of non-stop corporate work, where for months together I could not even afford to fall sick, suddenly the universe brought everything together in my favour. I had all the time to get therapies done, enrol for courses, read and learn. This is how the universe works; it is always waiting with a bag of goodies meant for you. When you decide to receive it, and when you decide to move out of your slumber, the entire existence comes together to prepare the platform. It brings in the right people, right situations and events, and pushes you forward ferociously, yet smoothly.

As I began knowing and discovering myself more and more, I was connecting the dots backwards. My suffering had vanished. It was only pain, and that too was losing its grip over me slowly. The best feeling in the world while facing a challenge is to know that there is always a solution and that too within our reach. Dr Wayne Dyer once said, "There is spiritual solution to every problem."

Even though the human mind is very complex, it is not very difficult to understand it. Like anything else, the mind too has its patterns. The mind is most restless when it does not know. It dislikes mysteries and feels uneasy as the unknown approaches.

Do you remember how you felt as a teenager when your parents decided to change your school? If you recall the first few days in any new environment, they were always uncomfortable. Sometimes the unknown is very scary to the mind. It is because it likes to work only in the known periphery, where it feels safe. It is so frightened at the thought of change that deciding to leave behind a toxic relationship, a dishonest person or a humiliating situation takes forever; till one day the universe delivers its punch right where it hurts the most, leaving you with no option but to change.

Till the time the mind does not know the details or answers, it is always in pain and distress. It is frightened and disturbed. The moment the mystery resolves, the pain disappears. There is one major challenge with the mind, and that is—it will not let you know much. It is terrified of anything new, even knowing! We hardly know our mind, and that is the root cause of mankind's suffering, all the maya and illusions. Our mind creates chaos in its sincere and obsessive effort to protect us from any imaginable harm. Its non-stop work to keep us safe from any possible harm, hurt or humiliation causes more of it. Our mind is a part of the collective consciousness—it is not only yours or mine but a collective pool of information from forever. Even though it has everything it needs to lead us to a free-spirited existence, the hurt and the memories have made it a slave to its past pain.

To elucidate this further, I must reiterate that the mind is not capable of knowing or remembering what it has never experienced before and that it too is governed by the 'Universal Laws.' One such powerful yet secondary law is the 'Law of Attraction.'

This Law has three basic principles:
- Like attracts like.
- What you focus on becomes stronger.
- Your thoughts become things.

What it means is it does not matter what's going on and what is the desire; the universe would match what you are. It is a universal law, and like any other law, it applies to everything and every entity. The mind is an entity with a strong frequency; hence, the law applies to it and matches what it believes in.

The stronger the fear and the anticipation of the emotion by the mind, the more aggressively the 'Law of Attraction' would bring us occurrences that would amplify fears, insecurities and threats. It is a Catch-22 situation with no escape; old patterns and beliefs create more of a known way of life. The drawback is that the mind lacks trust. The ego genuinely believes that no other being is bigger, better or more intelligent and resourceful than itself. It is convinced that no other entity is equipped enough to save you from danger. Its disbelief stems from the painful memories of the past.

Since it only recalls the feeling without its association to the cause, it is always on the alert mode as a result of wrong associations of happenings and assumed causes. The mind, paralysed by its ego, chooses to rather remain a victim than accepting the truth and healing itself. The attitude of victimhood has been formed by a very strong collective consciousness, which is way more powerful than our individual will. The good news is that we have the tools to move away. The day we decide to be the master of our lives and delve deep enough to recognise and invite our soul to take charge, we would have defeated the mind. Once you perceive and imbibe the meaning of life, acknowledging that there is more to existence than your 'EGO SELF' and its feeling of separation, you can turn your worst enemy—this extremely capable, powerful machine—your mind—into your friend. Let me warn you, it would be like the naughty Labrador pet who would innocently chew on everything you possess, and yet give you that 'I have done nothing look' each time you caught it red-handed!

When you begin to tame your mind, you start enjoying a loving relationship with it, provided you keep all your six senses open and empty, developing a few more, if possible.

With more reading, therapies and introspection, my mind was calming down. I was finding pieces of the puzzle and putting them together. Each knot undone was a relief, and a new sense of non-ambitious achievement was becoming a part of my life. I found this was the secret of co-creation. There is something supremely beautiful and serene about this connection with the 'Higher Intelligence.' Your whole being, including the ever-suspicious mind, knows that the answers are authentic, they are real and that they would work. A sense of peace as a result of being home and safe takes over.

Such is the beauty of deep therapy work that your soul, mind and body recognise the connection to a 'Source' beyond anything you have ever known—a genuinely loving, all-knowing source of energy or life or intelligence that knows much more than you do. You feel unwavering confidence that this trustworthy source would be holding you and leading you all the way.

For me, it feels as if I have been on a mission! A mission to know, to discover. After the first taste of this sweet nectar, I have been after my truth with a passion that has been more like vengeance; I didn't care how, where and when I reached out to every single person and place that helped me move forward, sometimes even pushed me down the cliff so that I could fly. I decided to take the fall because I knew someone, somewhere was doing it. I just knew something was changing, the force that was pushing and pulling me in the direction I feared the most was way too powerful, too mysterious, too exciting for me to give it a miss.

I use the word accidentally often, and by that, all I am referring to are the coincidences that I was unaware of, leading me from one clue to another, from one story of mine to another, so that I could find the pieces of my puzzle. My encounter with an understanding of the universal laws also happened in the same manner.

It was a Friday afternoon, and I had reached New Delhi to fly off to the United Kingdom for a conference on 'education overseas.' I received a call from the airline that flights to and from Heathrow stood cancelled till further announcement due to a storm in London. Disappointed with the news, I decided to do some retail therapy to feel better. I reached a mall where I happened to meet an old friend; while we caught up on the past seven or eight years that we had not met, she mentioned that she had paid for a workshop but was unable to attend due to some issue at her home. Before I knew, I had asked her if I could attend the workshop. I would anyway be in New Delhi waiting to see if I could get the flight even by Monday. That was my first encounter with 'Law of Attraction' a decade ago, and it was one of the best things I did for myself. I loved the subject so much that I trained to be a trainer twice, and till date, I am studying it.

I have come to believe that teaching the basics about how this universe works should be a subject in every school, and as a result, we would have much happier societies.

3

Know the Universal Laws

When you do things from your soul, you feel a river moving in you, a Joy.
—Rumi

Before we attempt to understand the 'Universal Laws', we must know the very essence of this universe, which is called 'Energy.' The essence that keeps everything interlinked and interconnected, including the universal laws.

There are many universal laws; though very basic, they are crucial information that every human being must be aware of and able to apply. I say this because it is pure mathematics. If you wish to work with a smartphone, you should know how to operate it. We come to this life wanting to live well, yet do it all wrong, totally ignorant of its operating system. Let's imagine the whole of this universe as a gigantic super-computer, with detailed and complex programming in place—millions of software programmes being operated through different hardware parts etc.

Our life patterns are the programmes or the language being used to put this whole design together and make sure the hardware, as well as software, work together. If this all-inclusive machine had a user manual, so that everyone could operate it swiftly and effectively without any disruption at its optimum level, then we would call this user manual the 'Universal Laws.' They form the OS (Operating System) of life. Here is a brief look at some 'Universal Laws.'

Law of Cause and Effect – Karma

You will not be punished for your anger, but by your anger.

– Gautam Buddha

I have always been very curious, even as a child. If there is one aspect of my 'Inner Child' still alive, it is my curiosity which has grown manifold with time. As a child, I always felt there was so much more to religion (Islam as what we had been taught in school), God and life. Thanks to my father, I started reading at the tender age of two-and-a-half years. He was the one from my soul tribe in absolute alignment with my thirst for knowledge. He encouraged me to read and study almost 24/7 from the time I remember. He also taught me and in fact, demanded that I shouldn't accept anything just because others believe or say. He made sure I asked the right questions, introspected and participated in debates much before I knew the meaning of debate.

Though a part of this wounded my inner child, I am now certain why my soul chose him as my father in this lifetime. For him, at the conscious level, it would have been a matter of pride; satisfying his wounded male ego after having his first son as a special child. My father could never accept my elder brother. It was too hurtful for him to acknowledge my brother, hence making me an over-achiever and pushing me to be ahead of my age would have been a means to cover up for his forsaken child (that is what he believed). I, on the other hand, didn't know why I was always in a hurry, always wanting to do more, read more, learn more. My rush to finish everything was rather abnormal. I would push myself till I fell sick out of exhaustion. For the past two years, I am trying to learn how to slow down; it surely has been the most difficult habit to develop and I still need conscious reminders as well as tough decisions to stay with this new way of life.

Till the age of 32, I never slept more than three-four hours a day. I would tell my friends I don't want to miss anything in life by sleeping. I believed it was one life after all, and I wanted to make the most of it. It was later when I got to know during a 'Self Mastery' workshop, somewhere in 2010, that I was working on behalf of my twin sister's soul who had betrayed me in the womb, who was never born despite the pact that we made at the time of 'Soul Planning'—that we would go and do the work together. The revelation was so shocking and also important that I immediately called my mother to ask about her pregnancy and my birth, to which she confirmed that there was another foetus which never grew beyond 40 days. (Just for the record, I caught up with her in this lifetime and made her do some work; I made her edit this book with me. Karma, you see.)

Preeti, my student and now, a very dear friend escaped my mother's womb and was later born in India. She went to a Parsi school, loves Persian muffins and married a man who had a Persian restaurant. Well! Absolutely nothing is a coincidence. Whoever saw us together, much before we discovered that we were twins, always thought we were sisters.

It was after that discovery in 2010 that my childhood habits started to make sense. I would read almost every book about the soul, psychology, mind, fiction and non-fiction. I would pretend I had fallen sick so that I need not accompany my family to the market or any boring function just to stay back and read. It was when my mother discovered books under my mattress that she announced to my father that I was addicted and needed professional help. If anyone could match detective 'Poirot' of Agatha Christie's novels, it was my mother. She set herself alarms to wake up at odd hours of the night to catch me red-handed. Next thing I knew was that I was clinically diagnosed and declared an addict by age ten; addicted to reading, solving Sudoku and crossword puzzles.

Today, as a 'Life Coach', I firmly believe that every single thought, word, or person in our life is there for a reason. Our life is nothing but a beautiful synchronisation of events that are planned to take us from one point to another, in the most purposeful manner to help us learn our lessons, evolve our consciousness, understand life and enjoy it fully. The only purpose of our life is to experience 'joy' and get so drunk in the joy of existence that nothing else would matter. The lives we live are often far from the Creator's reason for our creation. Something tells me we have got it all wrong. Somehow we have been made to believe that we are here on some great mission. We are here to save the world. That's what every contestant in a beauty pageant says because it sells well. We surely are here for a benevolent cause, a meaningful purpose, one that's simple and yet profound.

How I see life has changed, and how life is happening for me is so beautiful that it's compelling me to share with you everything that has made life so much more enjoyable. For the last two years, I have found a new prayer for myself: 'Every day, I seek to be more of my cosmic reflection, more of me!'

There was a time when I wanted to know what my life's purpose was (for almost the whole of my life). Like everyone else, I thought I was here to do something big, to achieve great heights, become famous or leave a legacy behind! Today, I know my greatest purpose is to be 'me'! To honour the universe's image through my expression of being, a hundred per cent of who I am supposed to be.

My soul is satiated in the joy and freedom of being me—choosing me and an ever-growing expression of me. If all other things happen too, that would be a great satisfaction to my mind. This realisation has changed how I look at life, bringing a sense of awe in every moment of life. It has also changed how life is happening to me. I am sure one year from now much would have been changed, yet again. The beauty of it all is that everything is only growing and becoming more magnificent as I learn to pay attention to all the details of what the Creator meant for me. I know for sure that we are here to live up to our fullest expression and be the most awesome version of who we were meant to be. Who you truly are is not a power/money/fame-hungry, control freak you! You are not here to do anything. You are here to 'BE' and let the universe do its job for you.

My mother always used to taunt me. She would ask in a somewhat sarcastic tone, "What is it that you are searching for in those books? What God forsaken truth is it that you want to know? Girl, let me give you advice, the more you know, the more pain you would go through. It's better not to know everything."

Today I know she was sharing old wisdom with me. My mother is a wise woman in her distinctive way. One of the things every person suffers the most is 'The Pain of Knowing.' When you see loved ones suffer, you may be able to see through the situation. Yet you have to sit back, watch, hold the space, be compassionate and patient, even if the whole of your being wants to scream and tell them to open their eyes, to take that one small step, which they have feared forever and sometimes avoided for decades or maybe lifetimes.

True compassion is painful, not helpful. You have to wait and watch. You can't get entangled in their karma, neither can you ignore their pain. You know unless they learn the lesson, the pain won't go away! People may change, situations may change, but the pain will only become worse with every failed attempt to learn.

Coherently, the universe is not personal. It won't favour some and hate others. It is in support of growth and expansion, and it is so focused on its evolution that it almost kicks you mercilessly till you learn your lessons. If anyone is suffering that is because they are resisting to learn the lesson. They are combating the flow of this powerful force called 'Life.' They are in pain as they are refusing to grow, thus, stalling the evolution of the universe by not playing their part. When we take cognisance of this truth and consciously move out of the way allowing life to happen as it is supposed to—to support you, provide for you and reach out to you—the pain disappears, creating magic. We just have to pause, intend and invite the universe to do its job. I know it sounds simple, yet 99.99 per cent of humankind is unable to follow.

Since the mind does not remember much, and if it does, it is not aware of it, understanding the universal laws and their application is vital to a joyous existence. One such law is the 'Law of Cause and Effect' or what we call 'karma.'

Unlike what we assume or are told, 'karma' is not punishment. The universe does not believe in reward and punishment. There is no God who is free, sitting somewhere, keeping an account of what you have done, waiting to catch hold of you in your weakest moment and spank your bottom. Neither does God think you are super amazing in any way that you should be rewarded. For all those waiting to reach heaven where 72 virgins would entertain them, I have bad news—that's just wild imagination unleashed some one thousand four hundred years ago to keep men in check. If this is the type of God you believe in, then no wonder life is such a big mess. It is just that simple; your relationship with your God is what would reflect in every other relationship of yours, including your connection to yourself, your environment and others. This connection establishes the very foundation of everything you make or break.

The law of cause and effect only echoes that everything you think, intend, say or do, will eventually find a way and come back to you. So, if you do not want everything you are thinking and talking about others or doing to others to ever happen to you, then don't do it. You may escape the punishing God, but you really can't escape your conscience; it is going to follow you to eternity and back. It does not happen because some God is sitting in heaven, staring at you, waiting for you to commit a sin, then catch you and punish you. He is no moral police.

The truth all religions knew but kept from you is that the basis of everything in this universe or any other universe is energy. Energy is everywhere, it is interchangeable, it can be transformed and transmuted, it can change from one form to another, but it can never be destroyed. It vibrates at different frequencies, no matter how far it travels and no matter how many forms it changes to; it eventually has to go back to its origin.

People are scared of karma because they have been told—'karma is about punishment.' However, karma simply is about the energy completing a full cycle and coming back to its origin. Our soul is eternal; it has existed forever and would remain forever. The body would change in each new incarnation, lessons would vary, themes would be new, but the soul remains the same. Hence it carries its entire force, acts, thoughts and words from the past into the future. How we clear our karma and move out of its cycle is simple—simple to state but tough to follow.

The only solution is to be aware of ourselves and all aspects of our being. By living in the present moment and remaining conscious of what we think, how we feel, what we say and do, we can take care of the present and any possible future karma.

Through therapies, meditation and service, we can heal the past karma. The most effective way of healing karma at all levels is through wisdom—the wisdom of knowing yourself, knowing all layers of you at every level; to know your light and dark and fully accept and embrace it.

In the Bhagvad Gita, Arjuna asks Krishna, "Why is it that I am suffering while executing this war and you are so much at peace? What is the difference between you and me?" Krishna replies, "We are the same; the only difference is that I remember it all." What Krishna meant was that he remembered all the lessons, was so aware of himself and his mission that he was in complete alignment with the 'Divine Will.' He was certain that he was being used as a channel for the greater good by something bigger than him. He knew he was not the 'Doer', and that there was something greater than him at play. Arjuna, on the other hand, did not remember the past, nor was he aware of his 'being.' He believed he was the 'Doer' and continuously thinking that maybe he was sinning.

Therapies have been the universe's way of answering my sleepless nights of prayer for wisdom. I was shown the past to remind me of many of my lives, my deeds, my intentions and promises, to help me recall who I truly am and in doing so honour others who wish to discover their truth. I was put into a fast forward mode, which not only made me see my truth but also satiated my thirst for knowledge. Initially, like most of us, I thought wisdom was about knowing others, what they do, how they do it, what are other beings of the universe, knowing other realms, why things are happening the way they are happening in the world and many such questions. This ignorance opened too many portals and dimensions of knowing, some not so pleasant to encounter. It was only after 72 days of silence that I realised—no matter what it is that I wish to know, the only safe and accurate place to find answers to them is my soul. That shifted my energy, opened the door to a realisation that's magical and indecipherable— something 'unknowable' unless you discover it too.

Suddenly many doors were opening, the pain was there, but it was no more painful. It was a sweet pain, like the pain you feel after a great workout session, enjoying every micro tear of muscle and the pain because you know it is going to result in a fitter you. I was getting in shape to co-create with my beloved Creator. The feeling has been grand, and it refuses to fade away. It is only becoming more and more ravishingly delightful. I thank the universe every moment of my day for the knockout call.

Everything I had read was now making sense. From what I have observed, most people don't know how to read. They may read a lot, but they rarely understand the essence because they don't pause to reflect. People read to gather information but lack awareness. They gather as much information as possible, even to the extent of chaos and confusion, not knowing what to drop and what to apply. We process the information we have gathered as per our perception, conditioning and belief system; hence different people take away different meanings from the same information, resulting in loss of wisdom. It does not matter how much we read, educate ourselves, attend seminars; unless our perception changes, our life won't. The only way to capture the wisdom is that we remain uninhibited and open, or what I call being 'mindfully empty.'

Therapies helped me dive deep into my subconscious mind, recall and perceive the truth. I do feel blessed and fortunate to be able to tap into this knowledge with the least effort. I was made to witness my being, as I am. Slowly, but steadily, I was led to a new way of being where I started to get a grip of my life. I learnt life could change. I admitted my mistakes and as a matter of confession, a few blunders too. I had seen, felt, and now every fibre, every cell in my body knew that the only person who could clean the mess was me. I had a powerful army with me—I (my healthy body), me (my now aware and cooperative mind), myself (my beloved soul which was on a mission to start afresh). Hence, I made a promise—a promise to rescue myself from my old self and move forward with a sincere desire to change and realign with my truth. I was all that I needed to recreate a life I so deserved. I realised how lessons and experiences repeat and why they repeat. I understood that the universe has a pattern and that each individual would perceive the same universe differently, depending on their Karmic baggage, their gifts, the lessons they need to learn and how they are supposed to contribute to the evolution of 'All That Is.'

It has been a long journey, as it has been for everyone else; much later, after many years of vigorous work on myself, directly and indirectly through my students and clients, I could feel a sense of freedom. I finally understood the meaning of free-spirited humans. The lies that there are beings/entities out there wanting to get me, harm me, humiliate me, hurt me; that there are enemies and punishments, hate and ugliness. I heaved a sigh of relief when I finally realised: 'the universe was not against me but for me, that life was happening to support me, that I didn't have to do much, but to move out of the way and allow the universe to play its magic.' All I needed to do was wait for the rainbow.

For a couple of years, I remained drunk with this flawless design, in awe of its simplicity and beauty and how selflessly it always served me in the best possible way. If only we were told the truth. If only religions would stop fighting to prove their God is more loving. It is sad to see how people are still lost. Even though I know it is all part of a 'Grand Overall Design', even though I know everything is always happening for the highest good of all, but somewhere there is this deep, intense desire of wanting to reach out. I don't blame anyone, we all are the result of the human-made systems which have turned our only sense of bliss and solace, 'The Source', against us and made him/her/it to be our punishing God.

When I learnt about karma, I was delighted to be in India where all religions talk about karma; however, it is interesting how one can destroy the very essence of everything. I realised that even though karma was much accepted and talked about, we had not spared it in its land. I remember when my teacher was explaining karma to us, she had so much fear in her eyes that her eyes seemed like table tennis balls, her voice and expressions were scarier than one of those 'Conjuring' movie background scores. I have always been a rebel, and though I have often paid for it dearly, the warrior in me refuses to die, to fear or to step back. This characteristic has helped me peep into the unknown, sometimes even into the scariest dimensions that are not fit for discussion in this book.

Every time I would encounter any teacher who would operate

from fear, my mind would zone out, and a very clear voice inside my head would say: 'Don't pay attention, this is not for you.' I would instantly feel light. This message led me to a vast study of karma through all the past life regression and ancestral healing cases I have witnessed. I believe I am a student of life and give credit to my desire to seek, and the universe's support for further growth. I was keen to know for my growth, and my intention was very clear; hence the universe kept opening doors and presenting me with new wisdom. My rebellious nature proved to be an added advantage. I never knew why I did not feel I belonged to fear or that fear belonged to me, but today the 'aware me' knows because fear is the opposite of faith. You cannot have faith if you have fear. Fear is not real. It is either your resistance or your ego causing you to believe that you are alone in this humungous universe, left on your own to fend for yourself while everything and everyone else is out there to get you.

If we understand our basics right, it is not so difficult to move forward. The first and foremost lesson to know is that the source of everything, including our mind, is energy. To decode our mind, we must understand energy.

Energy simply is. It has no biases. It is not subjective. It is always neutral. Since it has no mind, it carries no judgement.

Now read that again.

What do you conclude? The universe too and everything in it is neutral. So no one and nothing can gang up against you unless you wish to experience that.

Energy changes form and transforms. Its motion is given birth by intent that moves from one form to another. The mind bears and releases that intention and whose mind is that? Your very own!

Dr Wayne Dyer said, "If you change the way you look at

things, the things you look at change." What he meant was that energy follows the command that you give. The command does not have to be verbal; in fact the most powerful command is your intention, the way you look at your life. The universe determines how life would give back to us the fruits of our perception. People often judge each other or even themselves, assuming the hardships they are facing are because they have been evil in the past. That is not true. Sometimes just a belief, a simple association is enough to bring us the painful experiences. This reality is not linear; we only live it linearly.

Energy can never be destroyed. It only changes form. From water to fire, to air, to stone, to earth, to gems, to plants and human, and the cycle continues. This force only moves in ever-expansive cyclic motions, always coming back to its origin. However, like anything else, it too is governed by the law of vibration followed by the 'Law of Attraction.' On its journey back to itself, it gathers more of what vibrates at the same frequency. All those who feel/vibrate in the same frequency get together like a magnet, making the ball of energy bigger, more powerful.

This energy is ever-changing and ever-expanding.

Since the essence of everything is energy, the same essence is in all that is, and in us too. Our memories, what we carry, the theme of our current life, our gifts and baggage determines how this energy would function through us.

Keeping the above fundamentals in mind, karma, or in other words, the law of cause and effect only means that when you put the energy in motion through your intentions, thoughts, words and actions, you set it up for motion in a direction which would eventually complete its cycle. It would all the while grow and expand by adding all the matching frequencies. It would eventually move towards its very origin, that is YOU. That is why if you remain mindful of everything you think, do and say, you can not only change the course of your present life but also set higher frequency energy in motion for the future in your universe.

To help you understand this better, close your eyes and imagine a flat horizontal spiral, expanding out exactly like that of a ripple in the water while its centre remains the same. As the ripples go out, imagine the centre expanding, and eventually all of it becoming one big cycle.

***

4

The Universal Connect

Another fundamental truth we need to remember is: everything in this universe is interlinked and interconnected, including all the universal laws. No universal law can work in isolation. It is very naive to believe otherwise.

In many cultures, including Persian, they say your mind is your heaven and hell. Because we are all a result of the mind, the life we lead is the fruit of our actions and choices. There is no heaven and hell as a destination, these are just dimensions of your conscience. Both are very much here, always present in your head.

Let's also understand that universal laws do not work in a linear format, so it is not that if you have murdered someone, you would be murdered too. Sometimes though, your guilt might make you believe you want to know what pain your victim went through, and you might choose the same pain.

To give an example of a linear cause and effect experience, let me elucidate my case—the most recent amongst my past lives that I have seen. Short, sweet and precise, it answered a unique question for me.

When I was in class three, about seven years old, volleyball was introduced in our sports curriculum. I could never play it, extremely fearful of the ball hitting my eyes. As a result, I would either close my eyes or run away from the ball, and I flunked in sports.

My mother met the teacher and explained that I was much younger than the other kids in my class, and if they allowed me to play any sport other than volleyball, I would make the grade; the teacher refused.

Later, I had a wrist injury while trying to learn the game and was excused after producing a medical certificate. (This is how the body comes to the rescue and tries to tell us something is wrong. Wrist injuries sometimes indicate a pain beyond time and space.)

A few days ago, I saw a past life where I was a young (21 years old male) football player, probably somewhere in South America. I had big dreams for myself with the game. In one of the matches, there was a corner kick from the opponent team, and I jumped to do a head bounce; the ball hit me very hard in the middle of my eyebrows and the next thing I knew everything had turned black. The football blinded me! It explained my fear of anything hitting my eyes, and my trouble with sunlight in my younger years.

Interestingly, I was crazy about the game once. As a young girl, I would watch the World Cup or any football match until the wee hours. During my tenth board exams, the FIFA World Cup was on, and I watched France versus Italy match till 6:30 am; only after that did I leave for my exam without catching up on any sleep.

However, after finishing college, I suddenly lost interest. I would still follow the score but never watched a full match—an example of a linear carry-over of energy imprints. Same cause, similar effect but milder, because other than a dying desire, there was nothing else for me to learn.

But this is not how it always is. It is only this physical reality where we have the concept of time and space, and as a result, a linear reality; nothing else is linear. More often than not, souls have the choice to equal the exchange in many different ways. The case given below is an example of the soul choosing more ease in an indirect exchange of energy.

A lady approached me to understand why her father was insisting, rather aggressively forcing, her sister to get married for the fourth time. It was an unusual case, keeping in mind that they lived in a small town in north India, where people are very conservative about divorce and remarriage. The girl had been through three extremely abusive relationships, and each marriage had lasted less than a year. Now, within a month of her third divorce, her father found another match and gave her an ultimatum. She was being forced to get married and leave the house despite being emotionally bruised and mentally drained. Under medication for third stage depression, she could not even come to meet me in person—her younger sister had come to seek help. At first sight, one would have felt that either the father is insane or extremely cruel. But he was a doting father to the younger daughter who was sitting in front of me.

Since it was an unusual case, I agreed to take it up. When we moved back to the root cause of the matter in a past life, we witnessed that my client was an alcoholic father to a daughter (the present-life father was the daughter then). Having lost his wife during childbirth, the father (my client) believed that the child was a curse and his grief turned into alcoholism. In that inebriated state, he would beat up the daughter (father in the present life) for being ill-fated and the cause of his beloved wife's death. The father continued to use the child as domestic help and beat her up every night. During one such beating episode, he broke her back, which led to his daughter's death. Later, he too died a lonely death consumed by so much guilt, and his last thought was that he also deserved to be beaten to death.

The daughter in that life had carried the energy of fear—that each time I encounter this soul, I would be beaten to death. At the time of her death, she had cursed her father (the client), that she wanted to see him die the same way.

The curse brought them back together. Curses, promises and commitments are a big NO. One should be cautious of the language one uses while making commitments and promises, for the eternal soul carries them forever. These keep the souls glued to each other. These are the stickiest energy cords we create and become a slave to them for almost perpetuity till they are undone.

In this case, the soul carried the fear of being killed too. That was the reason the father in this life was persistent in getting rid of his daughter, whatever the cost. He just did not want the same soul around. It is interesting how we carry the energy imprints and feelings from one life to another with such intensity while we lose sight of the story and the cause.

My client, on the other hand, kept moving from one abusive relationship to another. In all three marriages, she was subject to extreme physical, emotional and sexual abuse. Her guilt, the curse and the soul's need to experience the same pain were getting her what her soul so wished to experience even while the mind remained ignorant. That is how heaven and hell are within us; we carry our punishment wherever we go.

In another case, there was an old lady, about 80 years, who was suffering from piles and extreme body heat. So much so that she had boils/skin rashes in all seasons. During the session, she regressed to a lifetime where she was a very beautiful woman and a *daasi* (female devotee) at the time of Lord Rama in India. She started sweating profusely, and the itching on the skin was unbearable. She was moved to the root cause of the heat, where she saw that she and her daughter in that lifetime (granddaughter in her present life who also happened to have skin allergies), were set on fire. She said they were milking the cows in the cowshed when they were set on fire by people who were staunch believers of Lord Rama (Lord Rama is a revered God/Deity in Hindu mythology). She mentioned Urmila's followers had planned the tragic death.

She was filled with so much rage that her face had turned red. I asked her what was going on. She replied that she had questioned and objected to Lord Rama's act when he had sent Sita (Lord Rama's wife) to the forest and had put her through the test of Agni (fire).

She had logical questions. Enraged, she wanted to know how a god could not know about his wife's modesty. If he was God, he should have known the truth. Even if Ravana had molested Sita, God should have been forgiving. She went on to say in such an aggrieved voice—look at these stupid people who follow him (she carried on for 2-3 minutes). Once she had vented her heart out, I facilitated her to let go of anger through an intervention therapy till she finally said—you know what, this is not my business.

I knew the healing was complete.

Through the right techniques, she was moved back and forth in that life, and certain suggestibility was done so that I could finally help her heal her piles problem.

I asked her to forgive and let go of everyone (though it was a tough task, I must admit). Piles are usually (not always) due to the fact that the person is unable to forgive and let go—the inability to let go of hurt or any stuck up emotion. Once she forgave, she felt at ease and filled with the joy of freedom (tears of joy rolled down her cheeks). Forgiveness truly is a potent healing tool and is best when you practice on your own. It was, by far, one of the most interesting cases for me.

Even though as a therapist, I knew more work is needed to heal the throat chakra and expression of the feminine, but I felt a great deal of release had already occurred. I feel so blessed to have met such an aware soul.

After the session, her daughter told me that they were not allowed to watch Ramayana (story of Lord Rama's life) or chant any of Lord Rama's prayers. They could never understand why their mother just did not allow it!

Our body stores memories of the past in each cell. In other words, the energy of our soul is present in each cell of the body. It is the most beautiful messenger of the soul, telling us exactly where we are going wrong. You align the soul, get rid of stuck-up lower frequency energies, and the body then heals effortlessly.

I am often asked, "Why should we suffer due to something that happened in the past? Why the suffering when we don't even know what happened? Why should the ignorant mind go through so much pain when we don't even recollect? How is that even justified?"

Well, here we miss the point that the soul is eternal. The soul is energy, and it is never destroyed; it follows all the principles of energy. The past, present and the future are all happening at the same time; the soul's presence is eternal, its essence the same as the ever-present, ever-pervasive source. It is the mind that has forgotten, the mind that is time-bound, and yet we live most of our lives, sometimes even lifetimes, trying to satisfy the mind—our ego.

It is the mind that wishes to conquer, to compete, to

control, to do, to possess, to prove and to create. The mind has a limitation—its very nature is the cause of its impediment. It has a limited capacity to process and remember information. It can only create from which it has a point of reference. It holds on to selective information in a time-bound manner, depending on the intensity of emotion. Bound by time, the mind feels separate. In the realm of the soul, everything is part of one source, and everything is connected. In the realm of the mind, anything distanced from its state of being, appears to be part of the past or future. The soul is aware; it innately knows once energy has been set out in motion, nothing can stop it, it MUST complete the cycle. The only way the cycle can be broken or transformed into another is through wisdom that is attained when the experience is complete. This wisdom does not come from reading books or listening to a Guru.

This wisdom has always been there, but you can only imbibe it by experiencing it, feeling it in every cell of your body, yet knowing this too is another aspect of the 'beingness' of you, NOT the whole of you. If you remind yourself of this all the time, you won't disrespect your being by concluding and discrediting yourself. You won't trivialise the vastness of your soul with the 'smallness' of your experiences. Awareness of this truth is vital, as it helps you stay afloat and detached from the happenings of your life. It allows you to watch yourself and your life as a spectator. In return, this conscious reminder works like a painkiller. Your pain doesn't become your suffering anymore. Your achievements would not fan the flame of your ego. In other words, you do not acquire this wisdom; you don't intellectually try and understand it. Your soul simply knows it deeply enough, for you to BECOME IT. That is when you break the cycle.

Siddhartha Gautam became Buddha because he became what he had experienced; he became the BLISS.

To understand the process, it is important to understand the nature of the Universe, Soul, Mind and Matter. The essence of this universe, as mentioned earlier, is energy. However, this energy is potential energy, and the only way it can be put into motion is through intention. So if we say energy is the life force—the soul—then the mind is that which puts this energy into motion. The mind thinks and desires; it is the doer—hence intention can only come from the mind.

This potent energy then is put into motion through a super-mind with its gigantic intentional force. The nature of the mind is to do, to have, to develop, to expand, to create. Since at the dimension of pure energy, there is no polarity, the supreme mind operates from growth, expansion and evolution.

On the school of earth, however, there is another universal law, the 'Law of Polarity.' It states everything; absolutely everything must have an opposite. So the good must have bad, the light is to be followed by dark, and so on.

The moment the Source/God particles move into motion and separate from the 'Unipool' of energy, the mind believes it is separated from the source, not remembering that everything in this multi-universal existence consists of nothing but the source. This feeling of separation and fear of survival grows with each incarnation.

In all my cases, there was a feeling of separation and rejection by the source, followed by—why me? Why did I have to go back down to earth? Let me make it very clear—there is no up and down, there is no higher and lower, there are different levels/dimensions of consciousness and existence, and they are all equally important in the entire cycle of evolution. Evolution is not an upward journey; it is an inward journey. It is going back from the outer cycles of the flat, horizontal spiral back to its centre. There is no above or below. There is only within and without! Without is always the reflection of what is inside. A closer look at your environment, relationships, etc. would tell you what exactly is happening within you.

Apart from working with my students and clients, I have had this gift of being able to work for planet earth, the motherland of India, and other beings from different planets as well as realms. Knowing the deeper truths of the universe has always been fascinating. In the most astonishing sessions, I realised it did not matter from which dimension, realm or planet a soul had originated, nor did it not matter how advanced they were, nor where in the hierarchy they belonged—every single soul particle eventually had to ASCEND to earth. I am using the word ascend and not descend on purpose here. We ascend to earth because Earth reality is the only gateway to the evolution of consciousness, and we are the lucky ones to romance it. No wonder we are considered to be the closest to God, the kings of his heaven.

Earth and the human body is the only gateway to evolution and salvation. By salvation, I do not mean you would be going back somewhere; by moksha or salvation, I mean going back to who you truly are 'within'—that's where the source resides. The religions and the Gurus tell us we have descended because we were not good enough. Don't believe them; you were so good that you were sent to earth and given a passport without a visa to his kingdom, the only issue is you need to find the key to that heaven, and the key is within your very heart; well, somewhere there.

There is no doubt that we are the chosen ones. It is not we have the key but 'We Are the Key' to final 'BLISS.' We have got admission to the top school of this existence. Earth is the 'Harvard of our Universe' and what do we do here? We watch soaps on TV, go to rave parties, get intoxicated with all the lies we have been fed with and lose the way.

As I repeatedly mentioned in preceding pages, the universe has patterns. You understand these patterns, and you can be in sync with its function, purpose and destination. Just learn the pattern, match the rhythm and follow your light. If Buddha could do it, everyone can. The mistake people make is they want to become like Buddha or others. You can't become one trying to be like anyone else; you need to discover the Buddha within and not become like him. Just realise you, your journey and the path to it is your responsibility; you and you alone can find the way. Your way does not have to be the same as Buddha, your technique can be different, but the destination is the same. By all means, learn all great teachings, be attentive and revere all the 'Masters' of the past. However, you need to master what's for you finally.

We are precious; the truth is without our active contribution nothing would move; the other truth is that we are always being pushed towards growth, there is no free will here, the only choice is that we can either choose to flow with life or against it. The first choice brings you bliss and the latter, suffering.

Many people misunderstand the 'Law of Free Will.' Nothing in this universe is forced, but everything is manipulated. No being would have ever been forced to move to earth. Some old souls choose either by their choice (out of a knowing not fit for this book) or by way of 'Divine Manipulation' to remain on earth and help the new joiners. For all the new-comers, the higher intelligence lays a beautiful, colourful, seductive trap.

The 'Super Mind' that has created this universe has its games.

It is doing everything for the sheer joy of creation and evolution of its creation. It, of course, is the master of its game. What is crucial is to always remember that when it comes to evolution and growth, it is merciless; nothing can come in between it and its creation. No matter how much you learn, understand, practice and believe you know, it would always remain on the top of the game. There is no winning for us here; there are only endless levels of this game. Exactly like one of those video games you play alone. It is a never-ending candy crush! The only way you can move out of the game is by deleting it. Well, there is a hitch here too, the operating system of life does not permit deleting the game, you must complete all levels, and unless you learn to master each level, you cannot move on to the next. The beauty is that the aim of the game is very selfless, it only wants to make you the master, it brings every possible situation, person, memory, past and present skills to facilitate you through each level. These levels are our lessons and experiences, which once completed, would free us from the feeling of separation.

We are in very different times today; the desperation of the human mind has reached new heights. The human mind is so capable of corrupting everything. Today, spirituality is being used as a tool of control. Almost every spiritual seeker I have met has asked me, "How can I clear my karma so that I don't have to come back ever?"

The myth around karma, free will, salvation, destiny, God and other such topics has caused people to feel as though being on earth is a punishment—they are on earth because they are not good enough to be somewhere else.

These lies have been fed to humans over thousands of years to make them feel inferior and less worthy. This delusion has been spread by power-hungry people and has now taken over the entire consciousness. It is a simple human psychology trick. Only if you are less, good for nothing and unworthy, then you would need a guide to take you somewhere. Mind you; even the self-acclaimed Guru doesn't know where. Do you think if he knew, he would be staying here to tell the rest of you about it? Why wouldn't he leave if the place he was talking about was so much better? The truth is most of them are lost too. Many are consumed by greed for power, knowledge and recognition. The difference between you and him is that he knows you are lost as well, but you are lazy enough not to want to do the work. That is what they have always cashed upon; your disbelief, lack of a sense of responsibility and your need to play a victim, a deadly concoction that makes people fall prey to fake Gurus.

They make you feel helpless so that you seek their help. The word 'help' must be deleted from our vocabulary—I do not believe in helping anyone. Whom do we help? One who is helpless, isn't it?

When you ask for help, you create considerable damage in your system. Let me decipher this for you. When you say or feel you desperately need help, you announce to the universe that you are helpless. With that you tell the universe, you do not have the power, you are not in charge. You don't know the way forward.

Every word has energy, how you speak to yourself and how you feel is what you communicate to the universe, and the universe makes sure you have more of what you are and how you feel (Law of Attraction). When you seek help, you are helpless. Instead, you can seek guidance, the same way there is professional guidance available for banking, wealth management or party arrangement; you can find expert guidance for your spiritual journey. But that is only guidance; no one can do the work on your behalf; you have to do the parts that are to be done by you.

You are indeed a powerful being, like anyone else, you just need to tap into your power by believing in yourself and accepting that you are who you are—powerful beyond measure.

The moment you let go of your need to be like others, you slowly open the window to your soul, which is here to express the vastness of its being through its unique expression. Just imagine if Picasso wanted to become like Leonardo Da Vinci.

The ONLY time any human being is powerless and helpless is when he believes so. The Law of Attraction then helps you create/encounter more such events and happenings to validate what you believe.

I remember when I was fighting my case in the court, there were times I felt extremely helpless, and the feeling was so strong that it almost shook me off my ground. That was in 2016—the issue was I didn't want to do anything illegal, and thanks to some people in the system, I knew the problem but had no evidence to prove it. I was helpless, after seven-and-a-half years of running from pillar to post, I could see no ray of hope. Those who were to deliver justice were themselves being so unjust. I did not know where it would lead to as I no more trusted the system. In May 2016, I received a call from FRRO, Chandigarh, again, telling me that my visa was cancelled and that I had to leave the country. Later, I learnt that the officer had not even sent my documents to the Ministry of Home Affairs, but I had no way to prove it. So, I had to move to the court and this time not against my (then) husband but against an entire system; the chances were dim of me even being heard, but I had no choice. It was strange, my citizenship had been approved, I was awaiting a favourable decision, and this news came like a shock. I was in a rage, furious with the corrupt system, surprised at God for being so unjust. I was aware enough to know what I was going through, not to curse or think anything that would add to my karma but I was hurt, like an injured lioness, and I wanted to fight it till my last breath. It was my next stage of awakening; the events that followed took me to a deeper side of myself.

I can never forget that day; I felt everything shake inside me as if an internal volcanic eruption and earthquake had happened at the same time. I didn't know whether it was acute anger or helplessness, but I knew something left me and as a therapist, I was quite aware of the soul loss. It was painful, but I knew I had to get myself back together. My lesson was being repeated, so maybe I had missed the bus, but I was fighting for justice, and I would fight it till the end. Yet, I felt helpless.

It was then that I met a so-called spiritual teacher who called himself a Shaman. He did not feel right from the word go, but there was a deep soul connection, and the helplessness was so overpowering that I did not trust the awareness.

My powerless state and his power-hungry soul set me off on a real-life nightmare of tantric exploitation at an energy level. Since I was operating from fear, I met a person who installed more fear in me; it was six months later when divine intervention kicked me back into my senses. I faced extreme spiritual and entity encounters; if I say he made me go through such intense work that I could see stars in broad daylight of the Indian summer, I won't be exaggerating. It took me 18 months of self-work to clear those six months of energy invasions. Later, not only I healed myself from his tantric energy invasions, but also helped a dozen of his students free themselves from unauthorised energy entanglements.

The helplessness is where life drifts away from your hands. No matter what you are going through in life, you must consciously remember and remind yourselves that you and only you have the power to kick right back and fight every battle. They rightly say God/Source gives you as much as you can handle. If it has trust in your capabilities, don't demean and belittle the source and yourself by feeling helpless.

The question is how to beat helplessness? How to hold on tight till the sea is safe to sail again?

I do have a solution for helplessness, one that needs diligent practice. Once you master the art, there would be no going back. It is called "FAITH". The only ingredients for this miracle formula are a cup of patience, a dash of self reminders and half-a-cup of the sweet nectar of trust. Put these together in the oven of your mind and what you will have is a life-time of self-empowerment cookies that you will never run out of. It will be your solution jar at every turn of life.

***

Book Two
Free Will and Destiny

1

The Universe is Precise

There is confusion around understanding free will and how it can work around destiny. People often ask how they can exercise their free will if everything is already destined. If we have a pre-destined life, then how does healing work?

Imagine your frustration in this scenario:

You are a foodie, but you decide to see a health coach on an impulse to get back into shape after your partner has taunted you. She makes you sit through a hypnosis visualisation with a freaky dietician who takes you to this imaginary five-star hotel where they offer a lavish multicuisine buffet. Your mouth is drooling over the amazing stuff, but you are aware she is standing on your head, instructing you to choose any food as long as it measures up to the nutrition value decided by her. You wonder if you can have your fill, at least in the visualisation, for God's sake! She reminds you she is doing it all to make your willpower stronger. You know you still have to slog it out in the gym, whether you eat the yummy food or just have sushi in your imagination. Somehow, you convince yourself how much you hate everything on display. You would have not lost a gram, nor would you have put on weight, if you had your fill during the process, yet you have to do it because your health coach is hellbent upon preparing you for the result you once uttered in her office by mistake. Not to forget the hefty amount that you have paid and the contract you have signed.

The universe seems to have done something similar with us. It has made us believe we are in charge. We are in charge of that which is an illusion, not that which is truth. We are in charge of the Maya we have created and not the existence as it is.

So if nothing is real and if nothing changes no matter what we do, what is this free will that everyone talks about? And if we do have a free will, why would we want to play an illusionary game where eventually only what the coach wants would happen?

The good news is that we do have free will. The scary news is free will is like an automated car with an invisible driver, taking you on a fast lane to a destination you have no idea about while you are sitting on the back seat with your hands and legs tied.

This universe is precise—have a look at your body. Trillions of cells work together, ensuring that every organ does what exactly it is supposed to do in perfect harmony with all other organs—enabling you to do all that you are supposed to do, even procreate another life. The same precision applies to our destinies; as a soul, you have no choice of not incarnating unless you have reached a level of consciousness where you can choose not to. That requires completion of all lessons of matter existence on earth and an awareness of the consequences of not choosing to come back in a physical body or choosing another dimension. Till then, there is no free will of not coming back, and we all will reincarnate. Just before each incarnation, each soul is given the free will to choose its lesson (we can choose more than one lesson), the experiences the soul wishes to undergo, and its tribe, which would help the soul with the best, easiest and fastest growth.

The soul seeks help from the 'Guides and the Councils of the Karmic Board' to know the best options available. It gets enough time (so to say) to review, analyse and identify the lessons it has missed in the life that has just ended, as also in its previous lives, so that the best possible option is dished out for the fastest evolution. This unambiguous plan is designed to perfection while every minute detail is taken care of so that there is no scope for error. It is called the 'Soul Plan'—the Soul Plans it during the Life Between Life (referred to as LBL) period of its existence. It is a blueprint of the life chosen. It includes details such as parents, name, body type; all minor and major incidents, all soul contracts, the theme, the gift, the soul tribe, even the colour of the eyes, basically everything. Gender is the only attribute that cannot be decided by the soul—it is predecided by the Source, because gender is governed by the 'Universal Law of Gender' and the 'Law of Polarity', for, the simple purpose of Masculine and Feminine energy balance.

Once the Soul Plan is designed, we are asked to review it, and are given an opportunity to rest in the LBL stage to prepare for life in the new physical body. Our destiny is the Soul Plan chosen by the soul itself.

Once in the physical body, we are under amnesia. We remember nothing. Imagine if we remembered it all, it would all be so boring—no adventure, no joy. There would be no learning either. The process of learning becomes fun only through the experience of hits and trials. The Creator/Source creates for the sheer joy and fun of creation; it does not create to achieve any target; so, if we remembered it all, there would be no element of fun.

How exciting does it feel when we learn a new game? Each time we get better at it, there is a sense of joy. What sense of achievement and completion do we feel when we master any task or finally win that game or lift that weight? Imagine how exciting it is when there are surprises? Our mind likes challenges and surprises; else, it gets bored very fast. It fancies the unknown, even within its comfort zone. It thrives on solving matters and resolving issues. It needs to be continuously engaged and reassured of its worth. The only way it feels worthy is by creating new challenges and then resolving them. This loop makes the mind feel superior. Mind hides its extreme pain of separation and imagined rejection by the Source behind this mask of superiority.

Since you have chosen and created your destiny, you do have the free will to change it, but this comes with a 'conditions apply' tag. And the condition is: "As long as you don't tamper with the rules and the result, which is learning the karmic lesson, and as long as you don't interfere with the dream of the 'Dreamer', that is you don't come in-between him and his passion for creation and growth, and as long as you are ready to bear the consequences of your own choices, you are free to change. The 'Creator or the Universal Mind' so enjoys variation and new experiences that you may change what you choose every ten seconds. However, what you cannot change is where this universe wants you to be; you cannot withhold its evolution as a whole. If you slow down or start going upstream, it either knocks you down or gives you one of those earthshaking calls that I got. You absolutely can't mess with its pace of growth.

The only time I have witnessed the universe withdrawing support is when you are slowing the universal growth. Unlike what we think, this loving universe has no mercy on those who slow down others and affect the collective consciousness adversely in ways that is not in alignment with the 'Divine's purpose'; those who refuse to move when it is time and those whose work is over. Souls who do the above have no place in the evolution cycle; they will be taken off the radar.

A few years ago, I got a case of a young man who was assassinated in broad daylight. He was a prominent person from a very affluent family. One of his female friends had contacted me; she had met him just a few hours before on that fateful day, and the news had come as a shock to her. It bothered her that for months after the incident, she felt him around as if he was touching her—freaking her out. Being a married woman, she could not speak of her ordeal to anyone. When she talked to me over the phone, she told me that he had guided her to me. She recalled that the night before she found me on Facebook, she had switched off her cell phone and gone off to sleep. When she woke up the next morning, her phone was on, and my Facebook page was open on her phone! She read a case study and knew she had to contact me. It's not a strange thing; we are always guided, but only a few of us notice it.

Nothing is really by accident, no matter how bizarre it may sound. When I opened this case through a technique I call 'Soul Macrocosm Drama', it became evident that what happened to the victim was because he was going against the 'Divine Plan.' I did not know what it meant at that time as I had never witnessed anything close to it. His existence had become a threat to many lives in a way that made the Source unhappy. His actions, sexual habits and mental faculties had become destructive, and there were hundreds of married women and their modesty at stake. I got to know that the soul was not leaving this reality and had led the subject to meet me, as the soul knew his time had not yet come. He wanted to know why he was killed. It was not his Soul Plan!

He went on to say he was removed from the earth before time, and repeated it a few times, forcing me to connect to the 'Guides' to get him his answer. The reply that came was a great lesson for my students who were present during the session and me. The Guide told him that he was removed from this reality as his existence was no more in alignment with that of the Divine Will. For me, it was profound learning; I had goosebumps all over my body.

Another myth was busted; unlike what we believe, the ever benevolent Source tolerates you to some extent. If you cross its path in a way that there is no alignment with the 'Overall Grand Plan', it would very joyously remove you from its map. Keeping in mind all the wars, terrorism, killings and political happenings, I still wonder sometimes…why him? But then I do believe that my tiny mind cannot question 'Divine Justice.' Such instances are rare; out of all I have witnessed, there were only four cases where the Divine terminated the plan, and each was uniquely different.

In another fascinating case, a lady contacted me; she had undergone eight miscarriages in less than six years. Each time the miscarriage had occurred during the fifth month when the gender of the child can be detected. When I took up the case, it was disclosed that she had had a pact with an 'Alien' being. The pact was that she would lend her womb to the alien soul who could come through her to experience being a transgender person. However, this was not the time or the lifetime. The soul tribe (husband and extended family) in this life was not ready for this soul agreement yet. If this had happened, many Soul Plans in her tribe would have been violated. Hence, each time the divine intervention would terminate the pregnancy. Then her Guide explained the Law of Gender to us and told us that the choice of gender is not within the premise of the free will of the soul.

It seemed that she was from the same planet as the alien being, who ascended on earth thousands of years ago; she had a promise of brotherhood due to which she would allow the alien soul in her womb.

Their work done, both her soul and her alien soulmate were reminded of the laws of this physical reality, resolving the issue. She later wrote me a thank-you note when she gave birth to a baby girl after 14 months.

What we call the 'Super Mind', or the 'Higher Intelligence', has only one purpose—to be 'Grand' in aspects of evolution and growth. It operates from total ease and joy, so if you feel stuck, have challenges in life in any way, it only indicates that you have slowed down. It is trying to tell you to check your pace or direction—maybe you are swimming against the tide. It is a reminder for you to check for 'Resistance.' Remember, you can only have a plan aligned with that of the 'Divine'; you do not have a free will here.

'This Universe is all for growth, all that you need to do is to match its frequency, speed and direction.'

I was told by a guide, through a client in her Life Between Life session that I must write a book. I didn't have the confidence then, and perhaps even now, as I am typing these words. I wondered how would I ever write a book? English is not my mother tongue. I don't know how to write a book and many other thoughts clogged my mind.

Today, I am still not sure why I am writing this book. I have this huge resistance I try to beat every single time I open my laptop. I dread how much the reader will laugh, get bored or think I have written nonsense, but I know—write, I must.

If I am writing this book, there are only two reasons: I can't be preaching what I do not practice, and to voice my authentic self.

If I am asking everyone to follow the divine guidance, signs and intuition, I need to do the same or I won't be authentic to myself. I have also learnt that it is not about the result anymore; it is not about success or failure; it is about being there, empty and willing, and allowing the universe to work through me. All that matters is my intention; the result can never be determined anyway. If only my purpose is clear, determined and is in sync with my soul self, and if I am doing the best to my capacity, it won't matter how the book would be perceived. It is about the JOY of it and not the response. So here I am, willing to be a vessel, taking my ego by the neck.

Our 'beingness' is important, but it is vain to believe that we are indispensable. As long as we allow the life force to flow through us, we are extremely important, like the water pipes in any building. The Source of life is flowing through us. Let's take this chronology of water and life force. Like water, the soul takes the shape of its vessel. Imagine what would happen when the pipes of a building are clogged. It would cause leakage, damage the pipes and eventually, the entire building. The place starts to feel and smell damp, and sometimes the wall or roof collapses. That is what happens to us when we are not an open and clear passage for life; we start to rot. We become a place of fungus and lower frequency energies. Whether it is art, a book, your parenting skills or your aspirations, you need to allow life to take you where it requires you to go. You should let go of the outcome while you put in your best intentions and action.

For a long time—precisely five long, long years—I delayed this book. I felt I knew nothing; so how would I write a book? As I became more and more empty, I realised a hard fact—it's truly not about me, but about allowing the message to flow through me. The level of the game is changing; for some reason, the Source has decided it is time for this sharing. Maybe it's time we put down the play of words and talk to each other most authentically without the need to impress. Maybe it is time for some myths to be busted, or for the play to become even grander! I know it is time to shift gears, and that it is always for the better. The pendulum has been on the extreme of the lower side of human consciousness far too long, and now the swing is taking us to the other side—the heightened awareness of our consciousness. Maybe it's time I stop judging myself. Whatever it is, its will is my command.

***

2

The Realm of Consciousness

Consciousness is the energy or life that is present in everything, whether animate or inanimate. Everything that has ever existed has the same consciousness or energy with the same capabilities. What makes human beings different from a stone or a plant or an animal is that we have an awareness of this consciousness within us. It simply means we can decode, analyse, segregate, value, include or exclude experiences. We can understand lessons and choose the speed of our evolution. No other being has the free will to choose the speed and means of its evolution, and also remain aware of it.

To make it more lucid, I need to add further that while a plant can experience people dying in a forest fire, it can by no means understand and decode the pain they go through. Since it has consciousness, it carries the energy imprints forward to its next incarnations, till one day, in a human incarnation, it would be able to decode the feelings of the tribe burnt in the fire. Like Google, it has all the information within but cannot feel or decode the information. If you search Google or YouTube and watch a video of a woman giving birth and screaming in pain, you can feel the pain but your laptop, even though it has much more details of the event taking place, can never feel the pain of that woman on the screen.

People keep arguing about plants and animal understanding the feelings, but it is not true. They only respond to energy frequencies; something that matches theirs and is pro-life causes them to respond beautifully while anything that's anti-life and lower frequency would make them respond negatively. When as human beings, we interpret those reactions, we decode them with our awareness of those energy frequencies and imprints.

This consciousness is a collective pool of infinite energy, and each soul taps into it as per requirement for completing its journey. Therefore, as we grow spiritually, we become more aware of our being and realise we hold the entire universe within us, as the universe holds us all within itself. We slowly become one with this beautiful consciousness and sail smoothly through all of what life has to offer by picking up all that we need, gratefully and gracefully.

The problem with our time is we are in so much rush that we do not remember we are supposed to be aware of our existence. We want a lot, we want it all, and we want it now. It seems life has become more about quantity than quality. We have the maximum choices human beings have ever had in the entire history of human existence, but we can't choose. One of my favourite teachers, Bob Proctor says, "People think they know how to think, whereas all that they really do is processing information and making announcements; they don't know how to think, neither do they know how to make a decision."

Perhaps, he is talking about just ten per cent or less of the population. We are living in a world where many options have been presented to us, but the power of choice has been taken away. Most of the population is under mass hypnosis. We are a hypnotised lot, programmed to 'Not Know'! We no more gather information; we are being bombarded with it. Like a tape recorder, our life is being continuously recorded.

I lived in Toronto for a short while, landing there towards the end of November. Almost everyone I encountered warned me about winter depression. From mid-December to February each time I would be watching TV, there would be either warnings from health organisations or advertisements from drug companies, trying to warn people about how bad the winter depression and flu could get. Being a hypnotherapist, I was observing how they are programming people to feel depressed and be ready for flu. I decided not to watch TV because I knew what exactly was happening; I neither got depressed, nor could the flu get me. It is what all the news channels are doing to us—making us believe this world is not safe anymore. That all Muslims are terrorists, and all Jews are still suffering from the Holocaust. That only America has the power to save the world and any country who says no is a bad country wanting to invade the whole world; and, we believe them.

It is important to understand how our mind works. Our subconscious mind, which is nearly ninety per cent of our total mind capacity, has a peculiar way of functioning; unlike the conscious mind, it cannot reject anything. It says yes to everything. It is the critical mind that filters the information that has been received by the conscious mind; the capacity of the conscious mind in receiving, analysing and processing information is limited, unlike that of the subconscious mind. When the information units exceed a certain volume, the critical mind breaks down and can no more filter any information;

the information directly gets stored in the subconscious mind. That is what exactly the mass media is doing to us! We are being continuously fed information that is breaking the filters, and hence we are being programmed to believe what even our conscious mind cannot recognise. Most of us do not even reach the stage of processing information; making a decision is an all-together another ball game. To be able to process information and make a decision, some level of mental presence, which we call 'awareness' is required. Unfortunately, we are the copy-paste consciousness; we are not even present while cheating ourselves of our right to know and choose.

Consciousness is the energy that exists in every being. Consciousness without awareness of it leads to no evolution. That is why human beings are the apple of the eye of the Source; we are the only beings with an awareness of consciousness and also a choice of evolution. That's the best gift the Source could honour us with. It is through us that the Creator enjoys his creation; it is through our choices that evolution happens. We can choose because we have awareness. Unfortunately, most people have gradually given this choice away. Every time, the religion, the system, the culture, the tribe, school, et al. made a choice on our behalf and for us, every time we followed others like a herd, never sat back and made aware decisions, we lost a bit of our awareness. Finally, we have come very close to losing it all, that is, if there is anything still left.

Everything in this existence is relative; nothing is absolute. The truth is relative too. Awareness helps us to know our truth, the reality that is for us would help us evolve. Awareness is the knowing that aligns you with your truth; hence, it is subjective even though it resides in all.

When aware, no one else's truth matters. When aware, you would always be blank, because unless you are empty and in this very moment without the need to have a point of reference, you won't be aware. In the present, you can't be in the past or future; hence neither belief nor truth will matter. When in the present, you allow the awareness to be present with you—that is what is present, that is the truth of the present moment, and that is consciousness in action.

During one of the 'Self Mastery' workshops I was attending, I learnt about my twin sister. What I witnessed made me identify many patterns, and some knots were undone. I realised why I had been doing everything a minimum of two times or even more. In school, I studied both Medical and Non-medical streams. Later, I studied Psychology and Business Administration. When I started knowing and reading about spirituality, I did almost every course and modality at least twice. I always felt it wasn't complete, and I had to redo to know more. Even today, when I read books, I study them. I can read and re-read a page 10-20-30 times. I only move to the next page after I have really felt every word in every cell of my body and then see if it was meant for me or not.

I had never noticed this peculiar behaviour and my patterns till that day in the workshop. It was very scintillating. I saw myself in the womb where I was helplessly watching another soul, whom I knew was my twin sister. She whispered: "Work hard, this is going to be a tough life, so make sure you do everything right, I am taking away all your distractions so that you remain focused and put all your energy in work." I then saw her and four bubbles of energy move away. Later, when I went back to the same memory to heal it, I realised she had taken with her, finances, romantic relationships, kids and family life, making sure there was no distraction so that the work could be completed. The next scene was my birth; I saw myself being held by the doctor upside down; he was patting me gently to help me cry.

What I noticed was that I took a deep breath, but did not cry, instead I felt: 'The human touch is so harsh, the world looks upside down; no wonder there is going to be so much work.' I had noticed everyone was smiling other than my mother, I knew my dad was absent, and he had lied to my mother. I knew exactly why he was absent during my birth. I looked around and was amused by all the display of emotions while the two people I had chosen weren't present for me. Very vividly, I recall that all I wanted was for the doctor to put me down so that I could start the work. My twin sister had told me there was so much work to do, so why were they wasting time and talking non-stop?

While connecting back the dots, it was interesting to see how those messages from the sister's soul governed about 33-34 years of my life. Looking back, it is evident that my whole life was based on those messages. Everyone found a strange thing about me, and now I know why. My grand-mother once told me that I was born with long hair at birth and that she found it strange that I had not cried before the doctor had kept me down on the table. She said my eyes were wide open, and that I was looking around, responding to different voices as soon as I was born. I have always done everything in a hurry, pushing forward even at the cost of my health. I rarely behaved like a child in my eagerness to complete the work; I grew up mothering my parents and both my brothers. I started walking and talking full sentences as early as eight months, my father taught me to read at age two-and-a-half, and I was sent to school two years earlier than the standard school age. My father made me study two classes each year. I lost my childhood, so I had to go back and do over a hundred 'Inner Child' sessions to bring back the child within.

There is nothing great about the kind of rush I have made myself go through, and it is a clear case of how powerful the messages that directly reach the subconscious mind can be. It is so important to introduce conscious parenting to young couples who are getting married and make them aware of the basics. The soul, and the subconscious mind, are always watching and internalising all messages and emotions at all times. Womb and childhood are extremely important periods of a soul's journey.

Today I am aware this was my soul at work. Tired of forgetting in each of my previous lifetimes, it came with a solid plan—that it would keep doing everything, again and again, repeating it so much that it would make sure there was no scope of forgetting anymore. Though the result is to forget all and just be the 'Soul to Be', the mind has to lose its millions of identities carried since the beginning of existence, and for that, it has first to remember all. Weird, but that is how it usually is. Only after recalling all that it has done, is the mind able to 'dis-identify' with them, allowing the glorious soul to finally emerge—permitting its 'Divine Spark' to radiate its light.

Many of us go around living our lives unconsciously (myself included), based on the memories of the past, someone else's story, or based on trans-generational beliefs of the ancestors that we carry in our DNA. Unfortunately, even when we step on this path of self-discovery, we still go on doing the same thing, we follow what everyone else is doing. We collect information, compare and compete, copy-paste, allowing our mind to take us on another round of self-defeating, time-wasting 'Ego Trip.' The challenge with the path is that the 'Spiritual Ego' is the easiest to form, toughest to identify, most difficult to crack and stickiest to let go.

True spiritual work is not about gathering anything—neither information and power, nor ego and pride. It is about letting go of all the accumulations. The 'Spark' already exists in each one of us; the 'Source' is already shining within. All that you need to do is dig deep, throw away the mud, dust the space within and polish the already existing gem. Let it reflect the beautiful light in its glorious form!

It is painful to see how human consciousness has been programmed with myths that create fear, pride and ego. It is a matter of great concern to see how completely deprived of truth it is. The truth is you are here just to experience life, not to become your experiences. Life is already happening at full swing, just be fearless enough to witness it.

We are conditioned to identify with every experience and become it. We are our sadness, anger and hurt, our victory and misery, our achievements and failures. The truth is we are none of these—we are so much more than that winter depression they so want us to believe.

You are so much more than your sorrow and your success, much bigger than the mother, father, wife, husband and all other roles that you are playing. You are so much more than the job or profession you have chosen (healers included), bigger than your feelings and emotions, and so magnanimous that one life cannot contain you. Yet, you allow those in power to make you believe that you are incapable and not worthy of taking charge of your life, body and being. You are here to witness temporarily, to allow another more expansive new experience to flow through you. Instead, you wish to own everything. People even want to own up diseases—they say my cancer, my depression, my success and my failures. Nothing other than your breath is yours, so relax. Let all these possessions drop so that you can find yourself. Let me warn you, you are so beautiful, so wonderful that like Alice, you may get lost in the vastness of the wonderland of your soul. Be watchful. Don't let anyone take that sparkle away.

There have been many attempts to make us unconscious, and we unconsciously talk about consciousness. Consciousness is as much misunderstood as anything else at this moment. The only way you can become conscious is by consciously watching every intention, thought, word and action. By reading this book, you won't get anywhere if you do not consciously sit back, introspect, reflect and understand why you have become so much of your experiences, why you have lost sight of your greatness.

Don't take me wrong—I am not a pessimist but a realist. I believe unless we know where the leakage is, we can't fix it. It is important to understand what and where the challenge is. If we get the diagnosis right, that brings us 60 to 70 per cent closer to the solution. Identifying our 'Ego Mind' and where it stands in the cycle of evolution is a leap towards resolving and the birth of 'Awareness.' Humans are the only beings with mental faculties and have an awareness of their feelings and emotions, which are the tools to conscious evolution. We are the only beings that have the power of choice; all other species have no choice in how they evolve. We can choose and re-choose every single option, the only beings given the privilege of co-creation. All other beings can only pro-create. It is this awareness of our consciousness and the power of choice that determines the level of our evolution. The idea is to be able to make use of this gift in a unique way.

The path is referred to as 'Self-Realisation' for a reason— it is about you and your truth. It is about you and your 'Mind', between you and your 'Soul.' What anyone else is doing, what practices they follow, how they meet their twinflame or how many hours a day they meditate has nothing to do with what is your best step forward. The journey is from YOU TO YOU!

So how can anyone else take you anywhere? All the 'Gurus' and 'Sages', teachers and mentors, can only share with you what they know. They cannot tell you who you are. If you do not know it, how do you think anyone else would?

There is no 'Law or Principle' that defines or certifies the same level of awareness, and that the application of same principles would work in the same manner for everyone. It is not possible because we all have our baggage and gifts of the past. This universe is about experimenting, discovering, exploring and creating. It is about change and infinite possibilities; how can anyone think that his or her way is the only way? That's very naïve.

Be aware and pay attention. Be determined and curious. Guides in the form of people, books and courses will come and go, but you can only do the work.

For all those who gave their worries to their 'Guru' to take them where they need to go—let me ring the bell. You are a lazy person, who is refusing to take responsibility of who you are, who is refusing to believe the Creator has created you in the same love and light as he has created everyone else. You are playing small, trying to put your trash in someone else's bin. You are in slumber. You are insulting the Creator by not believing in yourself, and not acknowledging your potency; you are creating chaos by not walking your path. You are telling the Source His choice of giving you His ability to co-create was a mistake. I don't care if you like it or not, whether you want to evolve or not—don't fail the Source's dream. The Creator, for sure, doesn't like it.

So how do we not become the experience? How do we remain a watcher and allow life to flow through us? Even though it sounds easy, it is not. We have way too many distractions at physical, mental, emotional and spiritual levels, which prevent us from remaining centred and aligned. To be able to witness life, you need to be detached from it. Many people mistake their emotional numbness or mental fog of indifference as detachment, which is yet another mind trap.

When I heard the word detachment, for a long time, I too felt I was detached, and you can well imagine the sense of achievement it gives. Later, I realised I was numb. Detachment is not stopping to care for what is happening around you. Some people mistake indifference, where nothing matters to them, as detachment, whereas in reality, they are just empty and devoid of love; nothing can fill them up. Some people have become so numb out of their pain that they can no more feel. They are zombies, walking around half-dead, thinking this is spiritual. Alive, dead or zombie, everyone is spiritual; we need to uncover it.

Spiritual bypassing is when people find solace in spiritual talks, books, etc. After a few years, when they can repeat the information, they become 'holier than thou' beings, and perhaps even ascended. Interestingly, they all have similar 'Life Purpose' too. The only reason for them being on the planet earth seems to be saving the world and doing evolution a favour, and honouring everyone with their—never asked for—gyaan (knowledge). These people at the conscious level know a lot, they just haven't taken out time to practice and apply what they preach, and haven't understood the crux of the matter. It is very easy to locate them—the 'New Age Gurus'! They often give unsolicited advice, always know it all, and make sure you know that they know. They will make you believe you are still work in progress while they have figured it all out. Till the time you agree with them and don't question, you are 'dear, darling and sweetheart'; till the time you offer support, understand their journey, you are 'good'—they love you for who you are! But, God forbid, should you press the wrong button and ask something that offends them (which is not so tough), then the other side of spirituality takes over—where rude remarks are a way of self-love, name-bashing is karma, and intellectual questions are your need for self-sabotage. Suddenly, out of the window go all the love and spiritual advice because they were never real anyway. Be aware of such kind of aware beings. This new species is breeding at the speed of light.

To step on this path, you need an unshakable desire, an infinite curiosity, an iron will, an adventurous mind and a compassionate heart. There are tools and guidance that would facilitate you to uncover your truth and realise yourself only if you are ready to search your soul with a flashlight of honesty and integrity. You also need a truckload of tissue boxes to wipe off the stream of tears. The process of dissecting one's soul is a sob, dirty, painful, but fulfilling drama.

***

3

It's All About Awakening

We have had many awakened and enlightened men, but the reason we don't know many of them is that an awakened man would never boast about his awakening. He has figured it out in a very different way. He knows his knowledge doesn't matter, is confident of his 'knowing' as well as his 'not knowing', and aware all that he knows and has experienced is nothing but merely an illusion of his mind. He doesn't become his experiences. He has established a connection with all that he has known, taught or believed in a way that nothing is worth talking about unless asked for, yet every experience is a matter of immense joy.

A truly awakened person is only interested in his journey, wholly detached from everything while never missing the opportunity to experience life to the fullest. He knows every moment belongs to only that moment and nothing can ever replicate it. Nothing would ever be the same, so he is an opportunist in the real sense— never missing an opportunity to feel the joy of life, even if the joy comes through the death of his ego. The pain of being in a human body becomes his joy too because he is so full of the very life he is detached from. He has become 'Soul-intelligent.'

Nothing can distract him from experiencing every moment and detaching from it wholly, always eager to live and feel the next moment more intensely and fully, without allowing gratifications or criticism to take him away from the real JOY in life. He is determined to experience life with the same intensity with which he is committed to attaining salvation, and that can only happen with complete detachment. This detachment comes from a deep sense of certainty and an unshakeable faith that no matter what happens, irrespective of pain or joy, why and how it happens, the Creator has his highest good in mind.

This level of commitment to one's purpose and life while being detached from it, only comes from a deep knowing that 'I am not the DOER.' That, no matter what the result, it has nothing to do with me because I wasn't the doer. Once you achieve this, you won't care about your role in the process or your position in the situation; the 'I' melts into 'Being.' Others' reactions are no more about you—you remain completely aware of who is talking at all times. You will keep asking yourself...is this me or my ego? Or is it the Universal wisdom talking through me? It is no more about you. To be able to see that, be open to seeing all of who you are, from every single intention to every single word and action. You need to be ready with a dissection knife at all times and keep cutting to go deeper if need be.

Our mind is the most advanced survival mechanism ever. It is continuously developing itself to cope with threats that only the 'mind' is capable of imagining. When not awakened, it works aggressively to ensure it is completely in charge of the battlefield. When we step on the path of awakening, the mind becomes passive, but it never gives up; it quietly continues to do what it does best—control!

As we move on our path, we discover different aspects of ourselves and become more focused on our journey to 'Self-Realisation'; the mind too is growing with you. It is becoming more and more sophisticated. However while it has slowly changed strategy, 'Control' it must. Hence, it will seek new methods of befooling you, as you are seeking more of who you are. To understand how your mind works against you, look around and see how the world has changed around you, the introduction of new ways of chaos and destruction.

During earlier times, countries attacked each other to conquer the land, there would be bloodshed, and they would take people as slaves. Gradually, wars have become more sophisticated—from guerrilla wars to nuclear weapons—and humanity has come a long way. Powerful countries do not get into a war but make two mindless countries fight and then proceed to sell them weapons and earn fortunes. Then there are the terror attacks—when governments do not wish to lose money and manpower in warfare, and they manipulate the resources and minds of people in the name of saving the world. Destroying and demolishing countries for a possible future threat, which for some reason, only the invading country can foresee, even if it has never taken place in the last two centuries, claiming all the while that they are doing everything to save humanity. Maybe humanity that has a different definition which we are unaware of. There are organisations such as the United Nations who fight for human rights—what is interesting is that they are fighting for those nations where it is the member countries of the UN which are the ones abusing human rights. We have come a long way while being blind-folded—as without, so within.

They have similarly kept the world outside chaotic and

unsafe; they have sabotaged our inner world with pornography, sexual orientation confusions, violent video games, social media, even positive thinking and spirituality. We are now intolerant of not only colour, creed and caste, but also nationality, religion, food, ideology and almost everything under the sun.

The mind, too, works on similar lines. From bursts of anger, hate and display of uncomfortable emotions, our mind also, subtly and cleverly, is always planning its next move. The next nuclear war within is to save you from your self. It often uses fear and lack consciousness (which is another form of fear) against you, and why not? These are the weapons of mass destruction in a way that you can be shaken out of your guts. The only weapon, the most powerful one of all times that you can use to keep a check on how you are faring against your mind is by continuously watching, introspecting and reflecting about everything in and around you—reminding yourself that everything has a message for you. Hence, whatever is going on outside of you is nothing but a reflection of your actual state of being. If you practice this simple tool, you will become the master of this extremely robust mind, and that would be your ticket to freedom or what we call 'Salvation.'

Our mind is continuously getting scaled up since it is a part of the collective mind; it is way ahead of us. We move one step forward, and the mind has run a mile ahead. The challenge is we have to walk alone and find our truth, and while we have help on the way and support by the universe, we are fighting the very same entity that is to take us forward—our 'Ego Mind.' Remaining aware of every single intention and thought is the way forward. If we are unaware, our 'Ego Mind' will have an overdose of spiritual vitamins, and we would bear the side-effects.

While on this path, remain vigilant; this is an adventurous

journey. No video game can match it, but every breath is worth it. Unfortunately, to an extent, my mother was right when she said—the more you know, the more pain you will have to bear. Earlier, I would see people with an occasional mask, during the 'Halloween of their Lives.' As we get to see and know more (including myself), I see most people having masks all the time. Imagine just how uncomfortable that might be. I see people with social, emotional and even spiritual masks. It feels sad to see us running from one challenge to another instead of uprooting the matter once and for all.

I was at a gathering a couple of years ago, when the host introduced me to some guests as a 'Spiritual Life Coach', and very candidly, he mentioned to them—the subject of your interest.

We talked initially, and after that, I chose to witness the conversation. It was interesting and sad, strange and uncomfortable, all at the same time. To me, it seemed that they were escaping life, thinking it was spiritual. We need to understand this path is not a substitute to life; it is not an activity we do; it is supposed to be the way of life and not a part of our life. It was amusing to see how they were using spirituality to run away from a bored-to-death marriage or an unruly teenager or their low self-esteem. They used detachment to justify their indifference, and lack of interest and action in improving their situation, to cover up their failed attempts at life. People use the term detachment to justify their heart's desire of wanting to stop obliging people because they are so tired of pleasing the whole world. And now, spirituality is used to run away from their reality.

Detachment is not about washing your hands off your responsibilities, not about being indifferent to the pain and suffering around, and not about turning your back on family members or hurting them with inconsiderate, unkind so-called spiritual comments. It is about doing your best, kindest act out of pure love while never crossing anyone's physical, emotional, mental or spiritual boundaries. It is holding a space for others to grow while they face their ups and downs without being attached to the result. Doing your bit without any expectations of any exchange, reward or recognition and still being okay if loved ones refuse to learn, change or grow.

One needs to become like that enormous tree beside the highway, providing shade in hot summer days to all those who choose to stand under it without ever expecting anything in return while keeping faith and being centred in our being and staying faithful to our journey. We remain detached, yet compassionate and loving. It's about being aware—of your purpose in each situation, knowing when and how to do what, and when to stop—while spreading goodness and believing in positive outcome at all times. It's about being able to see, feel, know, act and respond with heightened levels of awareness, without any prejudice or biases, whether positive or negative.

On a larger scale, it is about being sensitive towards the world and yet having unshakeable faith in the 'Grand Overall Design.' We cannot stop being sensitive because what is outside of us is a reflection of what is inside. When you keep faith that the Source knows its business, you continue doing your part to the best of your knowledge and abilities, always aiming for the highest good of all.

That is what we call spiritual, not leaving your family and loved ones behind to achieve unconditional love. How can you learn to love if you are rejecting what the Creator has offered you? How can you talk love or become love if you are unable to love in the best possible setup designed for you by the cosmos? How can escaping your situation lead to finding your truth?

Everything in your environment, including any illness, is what the universe has offered to you in your support so that you can move faster and with total ease. Your family, friends and environment are your mirrors; your sense of responsibility towards them reflects your sense of responsibility towards yourself and your growth.

There are all kinds of people; in another gathering, I realised spiritual talks were more of a social thing. You talk oneness, unconditional love and heart chakra because it seems to be a hot topic. You turn around and envy other guests' statures or finances. We must constantly watch what we are doing and where we are heading. One thing is for sure—you cannot create a new life using old mind and habits. The mind would use all concepts to its benefit. Another such concept which the court of 'Ego' would immediately hold up against you is 'Judgement.'

If you notice yourself for a few days, you will realise that you pass over forty-to-fifty judgements a day. They may be positive or negative. The type of judgement is not important; what matters is that judgement sabotages acceptance, kills awareness and blinds us to the truth. It affects the way we perceive love, and it causes a huge loss of emotional as well as mental energy. Love and oneness do not go hand-in-hand with judgement.

When we indulge in judgement, we conclude and announce that this is the only way things can be and should be, which in turn solidifies our experience and makes any form of change a Herculean task. We not only close the doors to possibilities and new changes for ourselves but people around us. We also refuse to allow the universe to bring to us that which could be better, easier, and more fun. In other words, we block growth.

Judgement is one of the worst forms of resistance. It completely distracts you from the truth. People think judgement is when they feel negative about something, but it can also be a huge positive expectation or belief. In my experience, a positive judgement is more injurious to the health of your awareness than a negative one.

Don't confuse judgement with observation or intuition. To explain judgement first—it is an observation clubbed with extreme, intense emotion. It usually creates stories around it because judgement needs approval from others to make the person who is judging feel good about himself. A judgement also can be an observation with an intense negative charge—the person who is judging would have enough reasons and stories as to why what he feels is right, and you must avoid that place/ person/food etc.

To give an example, vegetarian people will, usually, try to convince those who are non-vegetarian why being non-vegetarian is the biggest sin on earth, bigger than even rape or murder. Depending on their convictions and background, they will use anything—from cruelty against animals, slow or non-spiritual progress, karma or health issues—to not only support their opinion but to convince you. When they talk, they do it with such conviction that they leave you feeling guilty.

What makes an observation a judgement is the energy attached to it; the charge that is oozing out with each word and gesture. There is a conviction in their voice as if they are God on earth and know everything; as if they can see into eternity. They would do anything to convince you that what they say and feel is the absolute truth. Judgement is against the 'Universal

Law of One'; hence the mind seeks approval. It is the 'Ego Mind' that has this innate need for confirmations and approvals to feel great, especially when it knows it is fighting the universe.

A judgement remains a judgement, whether positive or negative; holding a positive judgement is a bigger challenge for those who wish to access their awareness.

Think about it, when you have a negative judgement about a person, job or situation, you are always alert. Even though this too closes doors to better possibilities, at least you stay cautious, you prepare for what may show up depending on how imaginative your mind is. On the other hand, when you have positive judgement, you are in a state of heightened mania—neither aware nor alert. People say that you get hurt the most by your near and dear ones. That's because you are conditioned to have a positive judgement about people you are close to, which does not let you be a neutral observer—the basis of being aware. It's only in a state of equilibrium that you can remain aware; when you are just in observation mode, neither positive nor negative. Just there, allowing everything to pass through you as you remain aware. It is then that you can catch the signals; you feel what's good for you and what's not. In this state of awareness, your inner GPS would guide you. Your emotions, not feelings, always talk to you from above. Emotion is energy in motion, it is this energy that communicates with you, but is extremely subtle, and you need to be neutral to catch the signals. Don't get me wrong—I am not saying stop being loving or positive. I am saying be loving but blank, be loving but detached, be loving but aware.

That's what Buddha teaches, to remain detached and yet compassionate, loving yet blank, an observer, a watcher. We think excitement is joy. Excitement is a physical reaction to a mental stimulant. It is a result of the secretion of hormones into the blood.

Joy, however, is a soul experience, and it has no connection with any stimulant outside of you. It is independent. Joy is a state of being that you experience, irrespective of what's going on outside of you.

To have no judgement, you have to be a keen observer. People on the path of spiritual progress, those who make every conscious effort to expedite and enhance their journey, even go to the extent of training their mind to observe dreams. To be aware while dreaming, in control of their dreams, too—this is called lucid dreaming. Being aware demands you to be a watcher at all times, even while dreaming, that is what Buddha knew. To be aware of all that is going around, inside and outside. To watch the feelings, knowing that you are watching and being aware of that which is watching you watch! How this watcher feels watching you watch. Sounds complicated? It is not—it just needs practice.

There are many layers of awareness, and the only way to master it is practice, without ever concluding. As Gary Douglas, founder of Access Consciousness, says, "Everything is an interesting point of view." You allow everyone to perceive life as they wish, you let life happen, and you remain open to surprises because you let go of expectations.

Having no judgement is like watching a movie. You won't develop a strong like or dislike for what is happening; there would be no attachment to the characters, whether an actor is a villain or the hero. You won't start characterising the actor; you know it is his/her role. You know you are witnessing a drama, which is going to end and the person would be in a different role in the next movie. You either learn something at the end, or it is just entertainment, or, maybe, a waste of time and money, but that's all to it. You won't brood over it for the next decade of your life.

When you practice how to remain neutral, you allow life to unfold with ease. You open your receiving. Judgement infuses resistance, and that is the cause of all troubles. When you drop judgement, you perceive people, situations and the process of life as they truly are. That's a blissful life, blessed with 'Grace' in every corner.

I am so grateful to the universe, all my students and clients, through whom I have learnt so much. I remember around five years ago, a lady contacted me for her child's phobias. Children usually are a reflection of their parents, and once I looked into the case, I realised that there was a need for certain changes in physical reality. The child wanted the father to be living with them—the only reason why the soul had taken birth was that the father happened to be the soulmate. The message was conveyed, and for some time, he became phobia-free. But it was temporary. After a year or so, there were different types of phobias. I was then guided to do certain work without the presence of the child or any family member. When we follow our gut feeling, it is then that the 'Grace' works through us.

Like the Ho'oponopono principle, I believe I am witnessing everything in my environment because I have a role to play. Or, better say, I am a co-creator of it; hence it is my responsibility to understand my role and change my perception of it for the situation to shift. So, I chose to see—how was I co-creating this, what was my contribution? Instead of working on it, I chose to work on myself, and sure enough, I had a major role to play. My extreme positive judgement of the mother had blocked my awareness. I could not see the root cause of the problem, causing the child to come up with new and much more intense challenges. When I dropped my judgement, the truth unfolded, and the healing was complete. This is how judgement blocks awareness, your healing and even process of life. We must learn to watch out.

A few years ago, I was a facilitator at a 'spiritual retreat'. There were other facilitators, and amongst us was a yoga teacher, a very charismatic man. He had a mesmerising aura around him; being a yoga teacher in all-white attire, and his command over his subject, had swept a few of us off our feet and left us impressed with the branch of yoga he practised. We all had long days of delivering lectures and meeting clients, along with other activities. By the end of the day, we would get together to unwind and exchange notes. (For seekers on the path, nothing is more enjoyable than exchanging notes, learning more. We read, eat, drink, walk, talk and breathe spiritual talks and subjects 24/7.)

One night, this gentleman joined our discussion and asked for a healing due to exhaustion. I felt uneasy and told him I would explain what to do since I was too exhausted myself, and it was pretty late for a healing. While I was explaining to him what was to be done, in the balcony of our room, he asked me if I could stay longer—an extremely awkward question which took me aback as I was not expecting such a direct move. Thanks to my gut feeling of uneasiness, I recovered almost instantly and excused myself and stormed out of the balcony. Later, I wondered, why I had invited such an experience and realised it was the universe trying to teach me about how positive judgement too can be an obstruction to our awareness. Ever since I have tried to be a watcher, this was the best possible way for the universe to awaken me to this vital knowledge.

People ask me how would they know if they have a judgement about a particular person or situation, and I suggest they keep a judgement journal for a week. All that you need to do is to note down every strong thought, and then find the corresponding emotion to the thought or situation at hand. If you do this practice diligently, you would be amazed to know how many judgements you have about almost everything that's happening in and around you.

When I conduct my 'Judgement Cleanse' workshops, by the end of the first week, participants are exhausted of what they are witnessing within their mind.

Let's also remember, we cannot and must not stop observing, it is not about never disliking anything, but it is about knowing what is going on in your head and being able to dissociate from it. Allow it to be a detached observation—a sign to guide you to what's meant for you and away from what is not serving you. Observing without the need to make it significant to a point—that would take away your awareness, and hence, your peace of mind.

4

Workings of the Mind

The Marvellous Ally and the Furious Enemy,

—Our Delusional Warehouse

Talking about the mind, most people mistake it with 'Brain', and they take it very personally. It's no one's fault; the ego has to take everything personally because it can only think of separation.

Let's understand the mind at a deeper level and how it works. Each time I talk about the 'Mind', imagine a formless infinite ball of energy that has no boundaries. Maybe you can even imagine space. It also would refer to everyone's mind because that's how it is; the mind is a collective entity.

Let me draw a comparison to help you understand the connection of 'Universe-Mind' with 'Brain-Body.' The brain is the hardware taking care of your Body (the limited part of you), and Mind is the software taking care of your Universe (the limitless, infinite part of you).

The Mind is the collective consciousness or collective intelligence mechanism of evolution. Each individual uses the programmes matching their new project—that's the new life or Soul Plan with the help of the new hardware (body) for an outcome, which is the evolution of consciousness.

There are billions of software programmes and games available; the same way, those many bodies are available. This mind has always existed and will remain till eternity. You have a choice to select, delete, cancel and reselect any programme you wish under three conditions:

You will bear the consequences of the changes you make.

The changes must fall within the 'Divine' desire of evolution of the 'Grand Overall Design.'

It must not slow down the 'Growth of Evolution.'

Your soul chooses those aspects of this vast intelligence—memories, soul tribe, name, physical body, et al.—which matches the end product—that is the evolution of your soul through learning lessons and completing the karmic cycles. The job of the mind is to keep us safe from all perceived threats, which may not even exist if we didn't have the mind. The challenge is, mind stores all information across time and space, and hence, in the dimension of the 'Super Mind', there is no concept of time and space. The mind cannot differentiate the beliefs that we need, it carries everything, and when threatened, it pulls out the files that have left the deepest impression, which are usually of misery and pain.

In an attempt to remain up-to-date, active, and the best survival mechanism for you, the mind is continuously producing the virus and anti-virus for its system. To test its capacity and ability to keep you safe, it continually creates challenges and resolves them, feeling it is still the master of the game. The mind gets petrified of becoming inefficient and functions in a 'challenge mode' at all times; it is always fighting itself. Mind's only and most disempowering illness is that it breathes separation.

Let me share with you my example of how mind functions

and how it can be an ally to the soul's evolution. During my self-work, I realised the theme of my soul has been freedom, clubbed with a karmic debt to the motherland—India. Due to the soul's past oaths and vows made in many lifetimes, in different roles that I had had, I had to come back and serve the land of India. My learning was to experience extremes and extents of polarity, and we know India is one of the best places for extremes.

So at the time of Soul Plan, once all these variables were decided, I had to choose the programmes that matched my soul lesson, theme and outcome. I (Soul) had to choose the best possible match from the collective consciousness that would have memories of lifetimes of extremes, such as Freedom Fighters, Sages and Spiritual Gurus, Authors, etc. I, then, chose a family that would help me reach the land of India—to move out of a dysfunctional childhood and have a relationship with a narcissist, who would help me experience extremes of rage, revenge, vengeance, self-sabotage. All this while I sought my truth—freedom, which made sure I remained in India to fulfil past oaths and vows I had with the land.

I was implicated in a visa matter without any fault of mine, which took nine long years to resolve. Each time I relocated from India—or to confess, ran away (13 times)—I was brought back. I even acquired permanent residency of three different countries, but my oath and vow kept bringing me back to do what I was to do here. I had to fight for my freedom for nearly nine years in a country, which is the second-largest democracy in the world (my theme being freedom). It not only sounds bizarre, but insane to think of it, but that is how precise the Soul Plan is in action at all times.

Do you see how beautifully everything came together to help me evolve to complete my lessons, exactly as planned by my soul?

That is how the mind comes to the soul's rescue during its journey, till the soul remembers who it is. After I realised what I had done at the time of Soul Plan, I had to find out what was the need for my soul to choose such a tough, complicated Soul Plan? What was my need to choose extremes? I know everything is brilliant; the toughest lessons usually have the most beautiful gifts hidden somewhere. If I could figure out the lesson and go after the gifts, the challenge would dissipate, and that's what I did.

Challenges are the universe's way of reminding us that we have missed our lesson. As I was searching for my truth, I had a profound 'knowing', by far the most important and eye-opening learning for me in this lifetime: "The extent of man's misery and suffering is proportionate to the size of his ego. Man's capacity to challenge the universe determines the complications of his soul lessons and the chosen theme." I knew I had to check the 'Ego.' As I searched for traces of ego in every act of the story of my life, I discovered there was more to it—a deep sense of lost trust. My soul had no trust in the Creator.

In my case, it was not just about ego; it was worse. It was a disappointment with the Source, feeling cheated and manipulated by it, so the soul had decided not to choose the plan.

From reading books, attending workshops, and from my work experience with cases, I have learnt that souls decide their plan with the help of their 'Guides' and the 'Councils of the Karmic board.' However, some souls believe their work is over, and they no more need to go back to earth—these souls are either forced or manipulated to go back. The same 'Ego Mind' is used to push them back on earth. The latter are usually old souls. When I talk of the age of the soul, I am not talking about time, even though that is important for the conscious mind. As I mentioned earlier, in the dimension of the soul, there is no time and space, so the age of the soul is measured by the experiences and lessons learnt, and how many karmic cycles it has successfully completed. I am talking about lessons learnt, remembered and fullness of existence experienced. Based on these parameters, souls have different stages of soul evolution, like we have age in physical reality. Everything that exists in this physical reality has an exact energetic correspondence or duplicate in the cosmos.

Hence the stages of soul age are counted as infant souls, baby souls, teenage souls, adolescent souls, mature souls, old souls and advanced souls.

It seems I belonged to the second category. When I was taken to 'Life Between Lifetime' to check for certain answers from the 'Masters', I saw myself arguing with the Masters—for some reason I believed my work was done. I could feel that I was the juniormost in that meeting; there was some carry-over work to be done, and because they believed I still had 'Ego', it was decided I would be sent back. I had no choice; it was forced upon me, so I refused to review the Soul Plan that was already in place by the 'Masters.' I remember saying whatever it is, I will do it myself. I felt so much rage and betrayal. My therapist had taken a picture of my face at that moment—she said there was a long six-to-seven minutes pause during the session. Extreme facial expressions of anger and rage had emerged—my face had turned red, ears looked as if the entire blood flow in my body had reached the ears and the veins on my forehead were swollen like they would burst anytime. My soul had been rebelling a perceived injustice.

I felt I was being cornered by the seniors and Masters of my dimension. I refused to choose a plan, the Guides were counselling me, and it seemed as if I could hear and feel nothing. All that I was going through was a feeling of deceit and treachery. I felt helpless, manipulated and choiceless. When I realised I had no choice, I told them—don't waste time, I will handle it myself, make sure this is the last time, make sure all is done and over, clear all my karma. I had refused all help, closed myself from receiving even before stepping into my lifetime; no wonder I had to experience extremes and no wonder my twin sister had to withdraw from our pact and leave the womb. One of the complaints of my friends and family used to be that I never shared my troubles, nor ever asked for help. Well, it is no more a mystery.

Another case of an extreme spiritual ego of the past that a soul carried and finally healed is a case of a young girl who joined my classes about four years ago. She happened to be an attention-seeker, would not care a hang if a class of 20-30 people were waiting for her to finish her assignment! Even waiting for her to ask precise questions felt like forever. She would never finish her lunch-break on time, would use every opportunity to annoy others by making them wait. Many a time, I could sense the desperation of other participants. When she became regular in my classes, people would ask if she was attending and show disappointment if I said yes, sometimes telling me that they would join the next class. Everyone wondered why I was so patient with her and let her do what she was doing while I remained a tough taskmaster with others.

When I met her first in a 'Family Constellation', I knew her theme was revenge—she was coming to the classes to learn forgiveness. More than anything else, to learn to forgive herself for all the dark lives of spiritual abuse her soul had—misguiding, misleading people, sacrificing innocent people and animals for the sake of 'Spiritual Power' and 'Ego.' The soul was so angry with itself, so irritated with the fact that it had not learnt the lessons over hundreds of lifetimes that it was now reflecting in her conscious behaviour, of which she had no clue. She wanted to take revenge from the cosmos and everyone; she was only in the classes to challenge another 'Spiritual teacher.' It was the 'Ego of the Guru' in her challenging a mediocre like me. I had recognised the drama and refused to let her drag me into it, I was patient with her because I knew how much pain the soul was carrying; wanting to heal, but having an ego larger-than-life, not wanting to admit the pain.

As we worked together, she slowly opened up. When the soul felt safe with me that there was no judgement and no challenge from my side, when it sensed there was no feeling of superiority, it was then when she could finally see her patterns.

In a breakthrough session, she saw that she was a male tantric in one of her past lives, who would ask parents to abandon their children and then sacrifice them. When the tantric's wife (current life mother) got to know what he was doing, she left him for another man (the male ego was hurt, and he wanted revenge). She then learnt of her connection with her paternal grandfather. She always claimed that her parents never took care of her, and she was closest to her grandfather. While working on her 'Inner Child' issues, she realised she had been her grandfather's wife in her previous life—a mother to her father. The grandfather had a wife (she) who died after a couple of years after bearing a son (her father). The grandmother died when the son was just two years old, and later the grandfather married another woman and had two more children.

The soul was so in love with the husband that it came as the grandchild to the husband. But her parents completely neglected her, because she had to experience the pain of abandonment, which as a tantric, the soul had made many children undergo— the pain of being forgotten by her parents, one of which was her son from the immediate past life, and another was a betraying wife from the tantric lifetime. Her pain was so grave that she always talked ill about her parents in all my classes, and how she was a victim, how they never cared for her. As per her 'Soul plan', these would have been the only combination of people who would have pushed her towards seeing her truth, forgiving herself and finally, learning the lesson.

The life we choose, including the people and situations, is a result of who we are and not what we desire. It is this fundamental truth which is the key to awakening. Reminding ourselves of the fact that we are not just the physical body, neither the name we carry nor the mind, is the best tool of not only spiritual advancement but also is the doorway to worldly abundance.

The 'Universal Law of Attraction' brings to us what we are and not what we desire. We must remember that we are the sum-total of our past, all that we have ever been, and that is what determines our vibration. If we carry residues of anger, hate, injustice, fear, there would be people and situations that would help us have more of what we are in our life. It is not just a saying; it is based on the 'Universal Law of Vibration' which governs the 'Law of Attraction.'

That is why just staying positive is not enough; you need to BECOME IT. You need to realise your beauty by cleaning the residue of hate, shame, anger, regret and resentment. For example, if we say this universe is aligned with growth, and if you can't see others growing, then you cannot grow either because your frequency is not matching that of growth for all.

Remember, this reality is not a linear existence—it is not necessary for what you do or think, to happen the same way as you assume or believe. There can be millions of possibilities and ways to carry out what is to be done. The only way to determine that we won't go wrong is by having clear intentions, which does not guarantee the outcome but puts the energy in the right direction. You must have heard a well-known saying: 'All that starts well ends well.' It means putting your best foot forward in all that you do, keeping up with the right intent. The dimension of 'Spirit' works on intention and not the outcome. Whereas, since the entire human system is programmed around 'reward and punishment' for the outcome, our world today looks chaotic and is turned upside-down.

5

Being a Victim

Why do people choose to remain a 'victim'? We are always dealing with certain challenges at any given point of time; some we can handle, and some handle us. I usually get to meet the second category of people who feel their life is getting consumed by their challenges, and they can't possibly find a way out. Every single person who is in pain, including my old self, is always delusional about being a victim of circumstances. They have a wide range of blames, from people to other beings and even God. Most people usually have a football ground of blamegame and keep passing the ball to everything on that ground. Initially, it pained me to see so much injustice and suffering, but today I can write it on the wall that 'Being a victim is a sign of resistance.'

A majority of people who seek help initially demand a change in the environment that includes people around them. They believe they are the grieving party and the aware ones, hence everyone else, needs a treatment. It is no one's fault. We have all been told from times immemorial that someone else is responsible for our happiness as well as sadness. We have been taught to wash our hands off life through every single system man has created. Thanks to our social conditioning, religious teachings, which don't even allow us to think for ourselves, and Godmen, who tell us that they will set our lives right, we have forgotten what it means to live a life.

Once clients start working on themselves, they realise that the actual cause is within them. At this stage, most people disappear from the scene; it is too much work—less than five per cent of people continue with healing. Initially, I could not understand why someone wouldn't want to take charge of his or her life and set it right, especially after knowing that the solution was within reach. I would find it absurd that people were not choosing to improve their life conditions, especially after becoming aware that they had the power to choose differently. When I realised that I was the Creator of my life, and I was the only one who could change it, I felt free and empowered. For me, that was the most emancipating piece of information I had ever known. Knowing you have the power to rectify not only the present but the past and the future, unshackles you from the chains of suffering, and yet many don't choose it. Isn't it strange?

This behaviour used to baffle me. It would even anger me sometimes to watch people choosing to remain dispirited victims. The Kurd (my ancestors are from west Iran's warrior tribe hailing from Kurdistan) warrior in me could not relate to the choice of weakness and helplessness. Later, I realised that they were being beaten by resistance. I no more get surprised or angry; I simply refuse the case. I understand that I am not the saviour of the world. Since I am one hundred per cent responsible for my own life and my energy, hence I refuse even an iota of energy of resistance in my universe. I will work with them when they are ready, but not when they deny life. As my profession and my knowing has grown, I have become extremely patient with those who, at least at a conscious level, are willing to heal and create a better life. I am kind and compassionate, tolerant and patient, even if I know that at a soul/subconscious level, there are agendas and resistance. On the other hand, I have grown somewhat short-fused and uncomfortable with those who do not wish to budge and have a facade even at the conscious level.

Choosing to remain a victim is having a continuous negative, one-sided dialogue with the universe; declaring that I am in resistance and not ready to change anything. I am going to remain miserable and indulge in self-pity and self-subversion to show you that God is good for nothing, and the universe is unjust. 'The Poor Me' attitude is what I have no mercy for. If you refuse to help yourself and take charge of your life, who would? Why should even God help you? How can God or anyone for that matter help you? Have you heard the phrase "God helps those who help themselves"? It is what it exactly means. The only manner in which you can help yourself is by being open to receiving, being open to seeing your truth, being able to allow the universe to intervene and help you.

The universe is least bothered about how much suffering you wish to experience; neither is it going to ever stop you from receiving all the joy. It is up to you to choose and then be willing to receive.

The universe is quite pleased and ever in awe of all that it is. There's an abundance of everything created in your support; an unlimited offer on all that there is for everyone in the universe's store, and the signboard reads—'Take your fill.' It all depends on what you wish to take. If you want to fill yourself up with sadness, revenge, shame, hate, etc., the universe would only say, "Please be my guest! Tathastu!"

If you wish to fill yourself up with love, health, happiness, success and grace, the universe would respond the same and shower you with all that is there. When you seek goodness, the universe responds faster as this matches its frequency.

The universe is ever giving; it never says no. You ask, and You shall receive. However, you receive what you are and not what you desire. In the subjective spiritual world, the language of communication is feelings, frequency and vibration; hence, no matter what you say and desire, you will only attract and receive what matches your frequency. Remaining a victim is an abuse of your power, abuse of the power of choice, which is your biggest gift. It has the energy of complaint. When you complain, you are non-appreciative, and when that is your state of being, you shall attract more of it. That is a state of demolition and disruption, which in return, would attract more of the same.

Most victims of any kind of abuse have traces of abuse left in them—physical, verbal, mental or emotional. In extreme cases, it can lead to some form of addiction, either substance, sex, food or some form of obsessive-compulsive disorder (though there is no blanket rule, in the majority of cases there has been an association). Spiritual abuse, which is very common in India, is the worst form of abuse. In the spiritual world, it is considered the darkest, most dense karma. The term is rarely used as very few courageous ones would voice their experiences for two reasons—either they get scared of abuser/s and decide just to heal this aspect and never try anything remotely connected to energy work, or they heal it, but their spiritual ego won't allow them to admit it. Even though I could not decode why the divine allows this to happen—even if it is for the mere experience, maybe He could have let go of this one—what I know is that those who indulge in spiritual abuse are the ones who are the most misguided of all. It does not matter to which dimension of consciousness they belong; they abuse because they believe in certain untruths. Mostly it is the greed for knowledge and power. In recent times, money and sex have been add-ons too.

Most spiritual abusers believe that through their practices, they would either attain salvation or would be able to have more spiritual power to create a different world for themselves. There seems to be insanity taking over them; the shine in their eyes is that of hungry wolves, the hunger for power and control. The excitement in their voice is nerve-racking and not nerve-soothing. The story starts from their greed for more of 'knowing', and along the way, there would be twists and turns, leading them to absolutely dark, dingy places. I have had cases of 'Masters' who started on a humble note, and soon the taste of power and fame took over, making them lose their way. There have been Gurus who were doomed and defamed. I have met people who knowingly chose the path of 'dark' for spiritual power and few who fell from the throne trying to maintain a self-image or even committed suicide, as they could no more move forward.

There can be different reasons why the victim would choose the experience. Some may have been the abusers and dark workers in the past. Let's remind ourselves that every soul has to experience everything to complete the cycle of evolution; sometimes, it is merely their turn to experience it. There can be millions of reasons; what is important is to be aware and not fall into the trap. We don't know about anyone's journey, neither do we wish to judge and conclude anything. However, you don't have to remain a victim; you can be a survivor, a fighter or a winner.

Spiritual abuse destroys the belief system, takes away the

victim's power and trust. It not only disorients a soul but a whole soul tribe for lifetimes together. Hence, the degree of karmic fall, to my understanding, would be beyond comprehension. In 2016, I met a spiritual teacher; very knowledgeable, uniquely gifted with what he did, which made me bypass my awareness once again. I was in awe of his knowledge and presentation of what he knew. It felt good to have met someone who knew what he was doing as most people on this journey seem to be lost.

Though something in the air was always uncomfortable, the positive judgement was too strong, overlapping my sense of awareness yet again. It was a dream come true; in fact, it was too good to be true. I felt I had finally found a mentor, a guide, a father I so missed until he contacted me for the healing of his family member. After he explained the situation, he mentioned something that made me very alert. After our conversation was over, he said: "Sahar, don't tell anyone," and then added, "Even if you do, no one would believe you." All my 5+1 senses were on high alert as I heard those words. Usually, everyone wants to keep their affairs private, especially healers and therapists; the secrecy is because they do not want to show the world that they need help, which is a highrise ego sign, but since it is too common, we all are quite used to it. In this case, it didn't feel that way; there was more to it. What he said was alarming. It was telling me that there is a façade, and it is so strong that no one would believe otherwise. I believe 'Divine Intervention' was at work. This sentence made me drop all positive judgement and wait. My brain was fully alert, ready to fight or flight. A few more similar incidents happened, till one day I had a premonition about the family. I immediately informed him. With all the precautions, the same thing I had foreseen happened, but to a lower degree, post which he asked me to do a therapy, which I do in extreme cases, usually when there is a matter of life and death only. Requesting for healing, he told me that his Guru had said that only Sahar could do this work; however, he had also said that when the work was being done, my assistants and anyone participating in the work should not utter a word. I found the instructions odd as the nature of the therapy is quite dynamic, and usually, no one has control over the magic that takes place. Still, I assured him I would take care of his Guruji's instructions while my knowing was telling me to remain heedful of the events.

This therapy was vital for me, I wanted to return the favours, and this was an opportunity to be of service to a mentor whom I so admired. A young person's life was at stake, so I made sure I chose two very trusted students of mine to join me. We started the therapy at the time and day we were guided. I had taken all the precautions to make sure there was no scope of error. I passed on the instructions that the client did not want a word to be spoken after we started. However, the cosmos had other plans; they had decided it was enough. Perhaps I had learnt my lessons, and I had to be taken care of. In the middle of the therapy, both my students told me if I did not allow them to speak, they could no more carry on with the work. I could see fear written on their faces, so I allowed them to talk and what showed up was the scariest and deepseated knowing ever. A series of terrorising spiritual experiences followed it—the start of six months of daunting experiences with dark energy work and tantric attacks. Those petrifying months felt like a never-ending period of my life, which made me initially regret my journey but the warrior in me came to the rescue and finally, I could heal the matter. It was, by far, one of the most consuming and fierce spiritual experiences I have had. Today when I look back, I realise that I had to go through that phase (it was the need of my soul to experience extremes) and I am deeply grateful to this gentleman for being instrumental in this growth. One of the most testing and exhausting times in the journey is when we come face-to-face with our fears.

The predominant lesson for me after observing most new-age Gurus and energy workers has been that most of them, and in fact, the entire human race is the prisoner of their self-image. People are most attached to their success, power or ego-infused self. They would go to any extent to maintain the façade, which of course, is the offset of their fall. In our field of work, at least, this can only happen if the individual starts to believe that he is the one doing the work. When this belief solidifies, it is an indication that the ego has taken over and all the great work is merely a distraction, another aspect of ego dancing its erotic dance of seduction and laying its next trap.

I have observed some people get carried away believing that manipulating energy (basically healing and energy work) is the end of the world. They feel it is a power or a gift only they possess. Some get lost in the praises and appreciations bestowed on them by others, and they start to believe that they have become demi-Gods on earth. We also have the shortcut enthusiasts, who for some reason, believe that through these practices they can exit the cycle of karma, not realising on the other side of this thin line, the father of karma is awaiting them—'The Ego'!

Let's get this straight—you may escape the human karma, but all that you are doing is coming out of the frying pan and deep into the fire. I am talking about the 'Master's karma.' Yes, Masters have karma too. If you study the Buddhist wheel of life, there is a beautiful message depicted. The 'Wheel of Life' is not just some beautiful work of art; it is telling the story of entire humankind and giving you clues of ascension and enlightenment. It is only through the human body that you can exit the wheel of life and cycles of karma. Masters and angels have their contracts with the universe. They have chosen a non-physical existence, which still falls in the cycle of karma. What I mean is that you only get out of a time-bound cycle to an infinite cycle of doing the same thing as a Master. The only difference in the 'Objective time-space reality' is that you have a human body, which is, by the way, your vehicle to finally bypass time and space, wheel of life and karma. However, in the dimensions of the Masters, they will have to find someone like us who has a body to do their work. And something tells me that it is not a very brilliant idea to keep working in a dimension where there is no beginning, no end.

We have another category of displaced spiritual people—the ones who abuse others for sex and money; this as an introduction is enough. The next category is the type influenced by Hollywood Sci-Fi. Quite entertaining! These are the ones that spend a lifetime learning practices that would teach them how to rob others of their energy. They need spiritual power to protect themselves and their divine self. They believe there are some dark forces out there coming to get them; in their mind, they are winning a *Star Wars* of sorts. The interesting part is they too are looking for salvation and oneness. Maybe, they need to be reminded that the dark and the light reside in the very same place within them, within everyone and everything, even if some dark buddies are searching for them; something in them needs to heal and not outside of them.

The truth is there is no one is out there to get anyone. No force which is outside of you is against you. It is your mind, your DNA, your past energy imprints that are responsible for the entirety of everything you go through. There are billions of you existing, both for you and against you. Whichever you give power to would win the battle. Your enemy is extremely powerful; knows you as no one else does. It knows all that you have forgotten about you; it knows every drop of your blood, every strand of your hair. It is mighty tactful because it is no one but YOU.

It knows every thought you have ever thought in your entire existence, every drop of tear you have ever shed, every wound you have ever felt and is going to press them till you bleed to death, but like any other great warrior, it has a weakness—the greed to know more. And that is your only weapon, the knowing we call awareness—awareness of the whole of you. It is a battle you are fighting against you! The most potent enemy versus the most powerful being in your universe—You. No other person's energy can help you. The most foolish mistake of all religions so far has been that they made you fearful of a God outside of you. And man has been trying to find ways to escape, manipulate or bypass this force outside of him. If they told you that your punishing God is sitting inside of you, if they told you that he would know your intentions before it came to the notice of your mind, if they told you this punishing God only punishes the cause of everything and not the effects, and that he is sitting inside, watching you from inside out, humankind would have known there is no point wasting time, as there would be no way of escaping oneself.

Man's approach has been so wrong; this is a battle you cannot win by attacking, killing or cutting out any part of it. It is a battle you can win by accepting and befriending, by loving through compassion and approval of the self. Love for the self with its many shades of grey!

***

Book Three
Beating the Chaos

1

Awakened Mind to Illuminated Heart

When we talk of being awakened, the first thing we need to let go of is the concept of time, space and linear thinking. Even though the universe is based on patterns, it follows simple laws and is always for our growth, but that does not mean everything happens in the manner we think or understand. Our 'Mind' is linear, our 'Spirit' all-pervasive and all-inclusive.

To be able to move from 'The Awakened Self' to 'The Realised Self', there is a huge distance to be covered. It requires diligent effort, conscious reminders and attentive observance. It requires self-discipline not of the kind that is temporary until you achieve a goal, but a constant push towards the most concrete wall of resistance until it collapses completely. The learning in the mind happens through logic and understanding, the soul, on the other hand, needs to grasp through emotions and experiences. The 'Mind' learns while the 'Soul' simply knows—when the lesson is learnt. The distance between the logical mind and the knowing soul is wider than the vast deserts and deeper than the deepest oceans.

It is the need of the mind to know and to have evidence. The soul just knows; it feels it. To allow the soul to know, you need to drop all learning and be open and clear like a blank tape, childlike. My desire is you read this book not from the point of learning, but a level of allowance. Unless you are open and receptive, you won't be able to get what I am trying to say. You would only understand what you wish to learn. If humanity had known how to read books, religious leaders would have never been able to misguide us. The challenge is we hear, read and understand everything based on what we are already programmed for; trying to compare or seek validation of what we know. If we do that, we remain where we are; there will be no growth.

Man's pre-conditioned mind has not let him see life as the Creator wished for him and experience it how the universe had designed it. The purpose of the Creator to gift him the awareness was for man to enjoy its creation, to move from one level of the game to another and have fun. Instead, we created so much suffering, so much chaos. We could never be courageous enough to let go of the need to belong. We were so scared of abandonment and rejection that we have tried to hold on to anything we got our hands on. The more man wanted to belong, the more he felt separated. It has become so bad that almost everything, from God, religion, nationality and even our food, has become a misunderstood concept, a means of separation, and a tool of superiority, leading to in-human acts. It is time bust some myths and uncover the lies we have been told.

The first thing you need to delete permanently from your world is the concept of right and wrong. There is absolutely nothing as right or wrong. Whatever is happening is always right. It may not be what you expected, wished or desired, but then that does not make it wrong.

There is nothing that happens without reason and for no

cause. Unquestionably, everything is the effect of a cause and has a gift in it. It appears as wrong, bad or negative to us because we do not know the brilliance behind those events.

When the gang rape in Delhi took place, it shook not only India but the entire world. However, nothing, undoubtedly nothing, can happen to anyone unless there has been consent in the soul contract. The victim and the victimiser would have agreed to go through the experience. Am I saying rapes should happen? Definitely not. Am I saying I could sleep that night and the nights which followed that horrific incident? No! It was the most gruesome news I had heard and the beginning of many more, but I knew there had to be something in it for entire humanity that my pea-sized brain was incapable of analysing.

All that I am saying is that we do not know the cause that led to the effect we witnessed, which made our hair stand each time we heard it. Maybe this happened to help the consciousness of the Indian society or the world to wake up. So that mothers who abort a girl child in hope of a male would wake up. Maybe this happened so that mothers don't tell their daughters to be careful, but check on their sons. Perhaps it happened so that people take a more active and responsible role in the upbringing of their sons, or that we, in India learn to have boundaries and understand there is a difference between love and lust. Maybe it happened so that the fairer sex wakes up and says 'No More.'

Or maybe we had to witness the extent of the fall of our collective consciousness. I just know that it was a sacrifice of the soul for the highest good of a nation and much more than I can fathom.

This physical reality thrives on chaos. It is in this orderly chaos that the manifestation happens at lightning speed, and evolution takes place. I say orderly chaos as everything still happens in patterns and in alignment with the universal laws. The micro-planning is ineradicable, unalterable and immutable. The macro planning, however, looks chaotic. It all seems very complex, but from the 'Multi-Universal' existence to plant photosynthesis, everything is happening with total ease. Unless there is chaos, order won't make sense. It is the 'Law of Polarity', and it is from this muddle that truth dawns.

This universe comprises of two poles of the same particle—the Soul and the Mind, the light and the dark. They are polar opposites and yet cannot exist without one another:

Soul is only Being. Mind is all Doing.

Soul experiences. Mind possesses.

Soul thrives to be free. Mind fights to be imprisoned.

Soul is detached and yet in union. Mind is attached and yet separated.

Soul is fearless and yet loving in its strength. Mind is fearful, vulnerable in its power.

Soul is timeless, boundless and yet aware. Mind is timebound and yet ignorant of its limitations.

Soul knows it all and yet is silent! Mind knows nothing, yet it screams.

Even though they both are from the same element—Source Energy—the mind feels separated, and anything that's separated from the source slows the vibration of the energy, resulting in form, whereas the soul remains forever formless.

The freedom of the soul is attained when it recognises its power and drops the all-nagging mind, which believes in doing and in doing forgets 'The Being.' It is amusing how all spiritual practices are also 'Doing-based.' You are asked to do meditation, to do certain forms of practices, to breathe a certain way, to eat a particular food, to grant forgiveness, to practice gratitude. We are using the same principles that we are trying so hard to drop. The reason for that is as we keep repeating, we become. The subconscious and the soul learns through repetition, and if practices are clubbed with emotion, then it never forgets. It becomes wisdom and stays forever.

That is the process, but I urge you not to remain stuck with the process. Intend to uncover your soul beauty and expression before each your every act. Have the desire to reflect your cosmic reflection in every intention, thought and action. We are told what to do and how to do because we need to be reminded—reminded of how to open ourselves to love, to become better, to do better. Sadly, human beings have to be reminded about how to love and be loved. The truth is you cannot be open to love because love is already inside of you, around you and everywhere. You just have to drop all the stuff that does not let you know and feel it. Drop the ego and love would show up on its own.

There is nothing you can do to be a better you, because there is no better you, at any moment in your existence you have been and are the best version of you. You just need to know, acknowledge and accept that. I am not saying you don't do what you do; I have been practising many practices myself. I am still doing a lot of stuff, but not from the space of 'I am not good enough.' I am scaling up my game every minute because I know I have this huge potential, and I wish to know the extent of my limitless, loving spirit. Nevertheless, we need to realise that it is not through any practice that we would find God. It is in searching inside that we would reach the source. Till the time we do not know which path is the one that would lead us to our very core, 'Try We Must.'

The nature of the soul is to explore—so that it can expand

and choose. You can only grow if you wonder, explore and then choose that which is best for you. You would know that your soul always knows what is best for its evolution. Through your feelings, it will tell you which direction to head in—just that you need to silence the mind to hear that subtle, loving, inner voice.

One of the major hindrances in our journey within is our belief in the concept of time. Since we believe in time, we are impatient. We are in the dimension of quick manifestations, but even then the result-oriented mind wants everything real quick. There is a colossal orifice that needs to be covered. The distance from 'you to you' is a generous perforation. Your ever-wondering soul wants to enjoy every breath and make each breath last a lifetime so that it can enjoy its very being. While the doer mind won't mind stopping to breathe altogether if it could help to finish task after task to reach a destination that it does not know about.

The mind's continuous effort to shorten the route has derailed us. Unfortunately, a few thought they knew the way, and they led people to no man's land. A few who knew the way refused to talk because those who really know the way, they also know it is only and only for you to know. Our greed has caused us to be manipulated, used and abused, at every level. Our laziness and lack of self-responsibility have brought us to a point in the evolution that the earth is calling for drastic energy shifts. When I was editing this book for the second edition, I was witnessing one of the most chaotic and challenging times in the history of human consciousness—the Covid-19 pandemic. Chaos, deceit and fear were at their peak while humanity was at its lowest-ever point of helplessness. Maybe it is a great reminder for us to realise that overdoing causes life to take its corrective measures that may not be too pleasant to bear.

I remember my father once told me, "Sahar, we have just this one life, it is not necessary that you must make every mistake to learn your lessons. It is always better to be aware and watch everyone; each person's success and failure has something to teach. Nature, children, animals and everything that is here has something to teach. You must have eight eyes and six ears to learn. Never follow anything blindly, but be a keen observer so that you can make aware choices, commit lesser mistakes and learn with more ease." It is advice my whole life is based on; I feel it's too much work to learn everything by trying them one by one, so many beautiful people are there to be taken as guides, absorb what's for you and drop what's not. Just do it with awareness, find out if it is meant for you and if that is your path.

***

2

Meditation and Spirituality

One of the most overrated and overly misunderstood concepts in spirituality is meditation. I have people asking me if they can practice meditation to awaken the Shakti energy, achieve Samadhi, change their lives, or attain a certain level of whatever they have in mind.

Interestingly, people want to turn to meditation, which is supposed to bring them from a state of 'Being', to an act of 'Doing'. Do you see the challenge here? Meditation is to help you learn to 'BE', to go within, to know yourself better. It is a tool to guide you into a state of just being. The results you get—all the experiences, all the different blissful encounters—are supposed to just happen. Regular practice of meditation would surely change your life, reduce your stress levels. It may even get you to a state of Samadhi, but those are supposed to be the side effects of the practice, they happen when you least expect.

So, what is meditation? It is a tool to become the watcher. Your monkey-mind is always jumping from one branch of thought to another nearly 50,000 times a day. Hence, some wise souls—the sapient seekers of the past—discovered that by focusing on your breath, especially when you breathe out, you would reach a state of no thought or what we call mindfulness, which is eventually the state of all-knowing. And here you go, setting goals even for meditation. If you have specific goals or have set yourself up for achieving anything at all through meditation, then please stop. You may go and watch Dracula movies instead. You have already defeated the very purpose of the practice. I don't care if you sit for 10 hours or 10 minutes, whether you do breathwork meditation, dynamic meditation or laughter meditation, but at least this one thing in your life should have no goal. Allow yourself to be a watcher. Meditation is about you watching your breath, becoming it and then slowly dissolving into your breath; everything else disappears, including your goals and the illusion you believe to be your universe. Then, 'knowing' unfolds.

As you practice, you too perish and evanesce. And then all that is you disappears into nothingness. That is true meditation. It may happen in one day, or it may not occur over a thousand lifetimes. It doesn't matter how long it takes, what matters is you flow with it and become it. If you set goals, it won't ever happen. You, for sure, would have wonderful experiences, you would feel on top of the world and maybe even powerful, but that would be another trap. It would be just another goal-setting activity you have got addicted to and perhaps obsessed with. In the Middle English dictionary, goal meant hindrance, limit, prison, boundary, and marker. So each time you set a goal for anything, you are only limiting the possibilities of your desired outcomes. That includes meditation too.

***

3

Forgiving is an Art

Forgiveness is for 'Real.'

"The weak can never forgive; forgiveness is the attribute of the strong," said the Father of the Nation, Mahatma Gandhi.

Have you heard of the Hawaiian therapist who cured an entire ward of insane criminal prisoners, without ever meeting any of them or spending a moment in the same room? It's not a story. The therapist was Dr Ihaleakala Hew Len. He reviewed each of the prisoners' files, and then he healed them by healing himself. The amazing results seemed like a miracle, but then miracles do happen when you forgive. He used the Ho'oponopono Miracle formula of forgiveness. I will share the four steps of this technique at the end, but before that, let's understand why every self-help book, author and therapist emphasise so much on this simple yet difficult step in healing.

One of the most paralysing peculiarities of the human mind is the fact that it knows how to get into an experience, the maze of senses and emotions, but it does not know how to get out of it. It seems to be a factory defect and surely put there on purpose. It is a characteristic which further disables the mind in many ways, so much so that the human mind, unless trained otherwise, can only create from same point of reference. That means it can only create what it has experienced before. For the mind—the human mind or the collective consciousness—to create from the point of nothingness is an almost impossible task.

However, it does not mean that it can never create something new, but the only way that would happen is when it agrees to step into the unknown, or pushes out of its territory and comfort zone, of which it is petrified. Usually, those moments are when the mind is working at a subconscious level. It is the mind's intrinsic nature to remain and operate in the known. The mind uses all its might to remain where it feels comfortable and safe. That is the reason why we have patterns being repeated in our life and people moving from one relationship to another similar one, or attract the same type of people and experiences. It is because the mind is comfortable in what it knows and believes it can handle. The same applies to our pain and wounds. If there was a way to measure the amount of energy and effort your mind consumes to hold on to pain, both old and present, to avoid an unknown new situation, you would not take a minute to change the aspects of your life that are causing you suffering.

While I was married, my mind was fighting tooth and nail to keep an extremely emotionally and mentally abusive relationship alive, until I decided to see a marriage counsellor. I ended up seeing four of them because I could not believe what the first three repeatedly told me. They told me there was nothing wrong with me, but my choice of marrying a narcissistic, psychopathic man was wrong. I could not believe it; after all, I had spent three-and-a-half years in a marriage where every day I was told and made to think that I was good for nothing—that I was a defective piece and the luckiest woman to be married to this super-precious, all-knowing, all-owning man. How could any psychologist, by just talking to me for a few hours, tell me otherwise?

Eventually, what worked was when one of them took a bit more pain than the others and explained to me the aspects of mind, which the psychology books in the syllabus didn't talk about clearly. She then told me that since I come from a violent, dysfunctional family, I managed to find a man who would cover for both my father's frustration and my mother's nature. I had managed to find both in one package deal so I could feel at home. Then she taught me to observe this triangle of Father-Mother-Husband and see if I could find anything in common. She also mentioned that even if I found just about 30-40 per cent similarity, it was a sign that I had come out of a frying pan and into the fire, and that the fire was from hell. The truth was she had a very valid point—my marriage was hell. I admitted it; I could not pretend anymore; I just could not bear to go through the nightmare. I was connecting the dots and realised the pieces of the puzzle fitted painfully well.

In the last counselling session, she went through my completed assignments, looked up and told me with a straight face, her gaze locked with mine, commandingly: "Sahar, just run." Then with a sense of pity, she said: "Sahar, if you cannot afford an air ticket (which at that point I couldn't), take a train or a bus or even just a pair of running shoes and run, but just do it NOW!" That day something in me shifted. I knew she meant business, and in that fraction of a second, I made a subconscious decision. Later I realised, I had been delaying the signs from the first week of my marriage; I knew it was a disaster quite early on, but my need to remain in pain, kept me there.

When I became a therapist and started cleaning every corner of my life, I realised how I had used my marriage to run away from home; digging a hole a lot darker and deeper than I had been in. That is perhaps the reason why people keep going back to their 'exes.' Pain becomes their home.

Forgiveness is a great tool to break this pattern of moving from pain to pain; just because we fear the new so much more than the existing pain, we refuse to budge. Some people (including my mother) react very strongly when I ask them to forgive. It is quite natural, they have suffered so much that forgiveness feels like putting salt on their wounds, but then salt is a cleanser, and so is forgiveness. The truth is forgiveness is your pass to freedom. Freedom from being stuck with the worst possible energy you can ever hold up to—freedom from hurt, from self-pity, from victimhood, from the wounds that you have been carrying. Freedom from the clutches of your past—the person who hurt you, the situation, and most importantly, from the pattern of your love-hate relationship with yourself. As long as you hold on to pain, and refuse to forgive, you will hate yourself for allowing the past to have happened to you.

When I say forgive, it doesn't mean you haven't been hurt; neither does it mean the other party did right, we are not condemning anything. It only means you don't deserve to be where you are, stuck and in pain. I am asking you to forgive because I am sure you deserve better and more. You are worthy of joy, happiness, good health, love, better relationships and more positive energy, more space in your heart and mind for a better, more graceful life. They say everything is abundant, and they are right. But your capacity to receive is limited; your energy is limited because at this moment in your life your cup-size is limited, it can only hold as much as its capacity and space.

Hence, you must choose wisely, if you want more of the goodies, you need to empty your cup of stale stuff. I do not know the size of your cup; what I know is that someone who has hurt you is occupying a great deal of space in it. It is for you to empty it, clean it of old, dirty fungus of the past, wash it, and fill it up with a double shot of life. And that is exactly what forgiveness does for you. Remember, forgiveness is for you. You forgive or hold on to that stinking garbage, and it would be only you who would feel the odour, your holding on won't affect them, neither change anything in their life; they won't even know you are hurting, and if they do, they may not care. Your holding on would only suck the life out of you and no one else.

The day you realise that you are precious and worth much more than you have ever known, you would forgive. The day you forgive, you are sending a powerful message to your perpetrator and the entire universe. You are telling them: 'I am moving on, I have understood the game.' You are announcing to the world that you love yourself so deeply that you do not allow anyone or anything unpleasant, who is not worthy of you, to occupy your mind and heart. You are telling the universe that you are taking charge, dropping the pain, and seeking your freedom—never allowing anyone ever to hurt you in that way again. That you are strong enough to stand your ground; you are ready to march forward, and now you want the universe to help you take a leap of faith.

A pertinent question comes up now: how to forgive when the perpetrator is in front of our eyes day in and day out? If the person is a family member who was supposed to have my back, yet she/he broke my back? Well, I have a formula: "Sweetheart, fake it, till you make it." At least start saying it, even if you don't mean it initially.

Our subconscious mind does not know how to say no, it cannot reject anything. It receives and believes everything. When you keep repeating something such as forgiveness, affirmations or any form of practice, eventually it masters it and starts to believe it. Once your subconscious mind believes it, slowly the body begins to recognise it too, and one day finally it would be done. You would eventually cross the barrier of self-punishment.

It took me three years to forgive my father; I started with just parroting the Ho'oponopono prayer of forgiveness. Initially, I could only feel an increase in anger; then slowly, the blocks began to open up; I started recognising his gifts to me. As I moved forward, after a while, I could see beyond my hurt, I could see through his pain. Then shame took over for a while. How insensitive and selfish I had been. I battled the shame until I recognised that I too, had been doing my best at that time. Then one fine day, the pain disappeared, and in its place, this deep, intense and grateful love entered from a space of knowing and compassion. I was free, and so was my father.

There are stages; you keep breaking through them one by one. Nothing happens overnight, whoever told you otherwise, lied to you. It needs determination, persistence, practice, prioritising and continuous digging as well as cleaning. We are dealing with a deadly combination of a bleeding heart and an equally muddled mind. It causes us not to see, not to feel, and block life completely. A similar process took place with my mother too.

The beauty of forgiveness is that the hurt, the deception, the rejection or whatever may be the cause, is replaced with love and compassion. It doesn't mean you have to become the best of friends or go back to your 'ex.' It only means your pain will no more enslave you. You will understand and realise that only someone who is in pain is capable of causing pain to others. It is such a delightful feeling when you are able to relate to everyone else and see life through their eyes, feel their wounds, simply knowing and acknowledging their pain energetically; it is for sure a heavenly feeling. It not only heals but uplifts human consciousness. You will realise that just like you, everyone else is longing to be loved. Everyone is yearning to be cared for. You will be able to truly understand that the person who hurt you, feels so devoid of love and is so empty within that he or she has nothing but pain to offer. Possibly, s/he did not know of any other way of seeking and begging for your love as well as attention.

Forgiveness frees you from your need of seeing love through pain. Your energy frequency shifts from pain-infused relationships to love and support-based relationships. You no more invite abusers because 'Law of Attraction' brings to you what you are and not what you desire.

Let me briefly share a technique for forgiveness—'The Miracle Formula of Ho'oponopono.' This very simple, yet miraculous formula is based on the belief: "As within, so without".

What Dr Len explained later was that in Hawaiian culture, they believe that everything that is happening in our life, whether directly affecting us, caused by us, or even just coming to our notice, indicates that we are the co-creator of that event. So our environment, the theft happening next door, or President Trump announcing war, if it comes to your attention, it is only trying to tell you that you need to heal an aspect of yourself, and that is what exactly Dr Len did by applying the four steps.

You will wonder how that is possible. Why would something, done by someone else, be connected with you, or how would your practising the art of forgiving would affect others' life or heal a situation not remotely related to you? The secret is there is no such thing as 'out there or outside of you.' Everything happens to you in your mind. Everything you see, everything you hear, every person you meet, you experience in your mind. You only think it's 'out there' and you think that absolves you of responsibility. It's quite the opposite. You are responsible for everything you think and everything that comes to your attention. That sounds harsh, but it also means that you can clear it, clean it, and, through forgiveness, change it.

Four Steps of Ho'oponopono Technique of Forgiveness:
• *I'm sorry*—Agreeing to be a co-creator of the situation and hurt.

As I mentioned above, you are responsible for everything in your mind, even if it seems to be 'out there.' Once you realise that, it's very natural to feel sorry. You realise you have caused it; hence you choose to uncreate it. This realisation can be painful, and you will likely resist accepting responsibility for the 'out there and not my business' kind of problems, but the truth is there are no shortcuts.

• *Please forgive me*—Asking forgiveness

It is most difficult to forgive ourselves, especially if the events and emotions are current life doings. Let's be honest, forgiving others still feels, " I am kinder/greater than you". So it is a lot easier because you are still blaming the other person and also admitting you are the benevolent one. It is forgiving the self that's a reminder of shame and guilt. So my dear, forgive yourself first. Don't worry about who you're asking. Just ask—PLEASE FORGIVE ME. Say it over and over. Mean it.

• *Thank you*—Gratitude

Say 'THANK YOU'. Thank the universe, the situation, the person as they have caused you to become who you are today. Without those experiences, you would not be reading this and wanting to be a better version of you. Thank yourself too, after all, you are finally taking responsibility for changing your life.

• *I love you*—Love

Say I LOVE YOU. Say it to yourself for healing yourself, to the person because of whom you are learning to forgive and let go. Say I LOVE YOU to the universe that has been patiently waiting for you to reach this day. Say it, MEAN IT and feel it.

When you forgive, you in no way change the past, but you sure do change the future.

—Bernard Meltzer.

***

4

Understanding the Word Called Love

It is a bit disappointing to witness that human consciousness has no understanding of its very essence, or what we call 'Love.' We have mistaken a variety of stuff for love; basically, our feelings, emotions or sexual desires have been misinterpreted as love. Love, in its essence, like anything else, is energy. Hence, you too are love, the difference in expressing it arises from your awareness of it. Do you recollect this truth about yourself, and if you do, what are you doing with this knowledge? Love is not something you can have or give. Sadly, we have misconstrued attachment, dependency, habitual co-existence, our need to be wanted, be needed or desired as love. I feel love should not be a verb. It should only be a noun because it is an experience, a knowing, it's energy, a vibe. It has no job to do. Like oxygen, love just is. Always! You are just not aware of it; you do not think of it. You only realise its absence, not its presence. Like the absence of oxygen makes the simple act of breathing difficult, absence of the awareness of love makes life difficult.

What man refers to as love is, in essence, the lack of it— man refers to his insecurities, fear of rejection, dejection and abandonment; his obsession with possession, having and clinging as love. He then tries to fill up this fear-based void with what he refers to as love, but he fails.

Love is the oxygen of existence; you breathe it. You can't get it from anyone else. You try to find love through someone else, but it would be as good as you being on a life-support system. Sooner or later the pipes would be removed and then boom— you are gone. Man's assimilation, rather his non-cognisance of this energy/concept called 'love', stems from his need to possess, his overpowering lack-consciousness and paralysing separation anxiety. Man's belief to love is to own, to have and to keep close. This crippling fear of loss, of loneliness, of being left alone with himself is what he has mistaken love for. He is so scared of himself that he is always looking for distractions. He feels so lonely on his own that like a beggar, he goes around seeking someone to fill up his void; someone to love him so that he can feel worthy. He feels so unworthy of love that at the slightest discord, he feels his world is coming to an end; that maybe his partner would leave and then no one else would ever love him again. That's why many commit suicide after failing in a relationship.

People claim to love their children, parents, partner, etc., but all that they do is control. They want their children to be who they missed being—to fulfil their dreams. They desire their partner to change and become who they want the partner to be. The truth is love CANNOT have any authority over anyone. Love is nothing but TOTAL ACCEPTANCE. It sets you free. It is 'Freedom', and freedom can only come from absolute acceptance. Love is letting the other person be, even if they choose differently. If you want to know how much you love another person, ask yourself how much you love yourself?

What is your self-talk? Have you accepted yourself fully? How much of you is in hiding? How much do you try to please everyone and keep others happy, so that they love you in return? Can you find out where you have hidden the liar you, the jealous you? Have you known and acknowledged the angry you, the greedy you, the lonely you, the shameful you, the hateful you and the depressed you?

Have you revised all your intentions? Do you acknowledge the competitor in you, do you speak your truth? Have you acknowledged the son who is irritated with parents, the wife who fantasises the neighbourhood man? What about the mother who is so exhausted with all the work that she wishes she had no children, the father who is so tired of providing and wants to just leave everything and find himself? The point is, can you see clearly and yet be so madly, deeply and completely in love with yourself after acknowledging who you are? Many blame their environment, background, parents and even luck for how their life has shaped up. It is difficult for them to be authentic; there are secrets of the past, agendas of the soul that make them believe they are not good enough. If you see and know who you truly are, and still believe you deserve abundance, love and bliss, then you have become love. And if you are love, you won't seek it. You will naturally attract it.

One can only offer what one has. When you love yourself, you touch that deep core of your being and allow your essence to flow. Love is about the flow outwards—you are so satiated that it just has to flow from you outwards—and the 'Law of Attraction' would make sure you attract what you are. Hence, love becomes a silent exchange of energy. You would then desire for others what you desire for yourself.

The same way you do not wish for yourself to be caged in the need-based, limiting feelings you had once mistaken for love; you would not want to make anyone subject to this imprisonment either. In the name of love, we have done great sins; in the name of love, we have destroyed people, nations and countries. In the name of love, we have sabotaged the truth and lived many lies. The love for your child becomes bigger than truth; the love for a lover bigger than another's life; love for religion greater than humanity; love for power higher than consciousness. Like everything else, man has made a toy out of love. We use it anywhere we please to fulfil our greed, to justify acts of selfish nature and inhuman encounters.

Long ago, when I was a kid, I watched an exciting programme—a study done on monkeys (monkeys are closest to human beings in the scale of physiological evolution at least). They kept a monkey and her offspring in a cage and started heating the floor. Initially, the monkey caught her baby and held on to the cage bars. They heated the bars, to which she reacted by coming down and holding her offspring in her lap. When the heat was increased to an unbearable level, what came next was shocking to watch. The monkey put the off-spring under her and sat on it.

You must be thinking this is an experiment on animals. Well, as a therapist, I have come across many cases where, similarly, people have sacrificed their children, partner, parents for their good. I am a believer of love but not a dreamer of it. Love is an orgasmic experience, it is supposed to bring not only your body but the whole of you to an ecstasy of union, but we have created more separation through it simply because we don't know who we are. Someday we must wake up. Unless we see and acknowledge the problem, we cannot possibly find a solution to it. And love is the only solution.

Some use love to fill up the void within that's stemming from lack of self-love, itself rooted in lack of self-worth. Some have abused the so-called love to justify their acts of supremacy, which is the counter effect of their inferiority. They permit themselves to be rude, to exploit others, judge people as not good enough, not adequate and unworthy. They exude the qualities of blue blood. Well, neither of the two is love. Love has empathy and compassion. Love is Aloha, pure acceptance and allowance. It does not judge, does not harm or humiliate; it knows no superiority, nor does it identify with inferiority. Love just is and allows the rest of the world to be. It does not feel offended; neither does it need to defend. Because when there is love, the ego cannot be. Love does not explain or justify, neither it accuses nor assumes. The third category of people, whom I call spiritual by-passers, is the most interesting lot. This breed of people is full of love under certain conditions, as long as everyone agrees with them. Their self-love can attack you at any time because it judges the rest of the world, and now you know where I am getting at!

Love has no charge; it allows you to disagree. It permits you to make mistakes, agrees to your feelings. The feeling, the knowing, the seeing, are all consensual, authentic and permissible. Love grants you the freedom to be who you are until you find a new version of you and as you do, it loves the new you too. It allows you to move back and forth, and both are perfectly okay. It holds the space for you, and yet it is sincere. It tells you what is lacking and how you can move, but it would never push you. It gently reminds you, lovingly nudges you and then walks with you; holding your hands, occasionally showing you the mirror.

I see parents who almost kill their children for performance, and I see them exhibit their children's achievements. That is not loving, but pride. Our children must do well, but why is it essential that they do better than others? We must understand the difference. In this universe, love is abundant, as is everything else. There is love as deep as oceans, strong as mountains, fresh as the breeze and pure as the morning dew. But, unfortunately, we have not got it right, somewhere, somehow we have missed the point. We are desperately trying to fill our empty hearts. It is not very difficult to feel the kind of love that is actually love. The secret is you need to first dig it out of you, then allow it to flow outwards; moving out of you, it will find the one who would match the frequency of it.

I once met a gentleman who very strongly felt that he loved me. He proposed to marry me and shared how deeply he felt. In his attempt to convince me how he could be a 'good deal' for me, he shared some of his ideas and dreams. He was a fine man, like any other person he wished to love and to be loved. However, his conversations made me realise a disturbing reality, that most of us have made love a business. It is more like, I bring X, Y, Z to the table and you bring A, B, C. To me this is not love; it is a calculation, a barter system, a negotiation of interests, investments and costs. A system we have adopted and follow so unconsciously that now it feels normal even though the consequences are emotionally dysfunctional societies. It is a business. To my understanding, love does not think. It is just not capable of thinking because it comes from the soul; moreover, the soul comes from it. It is untouched by the mind. It does not know how to negotiate.

To know love and find it, all you have to do is "FIND YOURSELF AND LOVE WHAT YOU HAVE FOUND".

5

The Power of Prayer

A few years ago, Amrita, one of my colleagues, asked me, "Sahar, how do I pray and what is the right way to pray?" She said she wanted to pray because it was only through it that 'Grace' would enter her life. I looked at her, quite baffled. I told her that my prayer was my daily conversations with the universe that I did it when I felt it from my heart as if I was talking to a friend, and I usually ended my monologue with gratitude. However, as I replied to her, I also realised that I was unsure if that was the right way to pray. Her question stayed with me for a couple of years. I wondered what would be the type of prayer that would open the doors of grace. I wondered if God had to pray, how would he pray? I was seeking—I asked the universe to help me know how to pray. Finally, two years later, the universe answered my question most profoundly. The answer came during a therapy session.

A medium had told a friend of mine that there was some foreign energy attached to him, meant to halt his personal and professional growth. Once the case was open, the foreign energy seemed to be a minor matter, as there were deeper issues to be healed. (The Universe has its beautiful ways of guiding us to heal when the time is right and the lesson is to be learnt.)

As the session commenced, we learnt that he had been a High Priest in his previous life in a king's palace, honoured and highly sought after. Even though he was of such stature, he slept and lived in a cave and meditated for 18-20 hours a day. A lady, who was one of the dancers in the same palace, was given the duty of serving the High Priest. She was a seductress, a joyful and fun-loving 17-18-year-old dancer, who could not understand the ways of the High Priest.

Her curiosity took over, and she decided to seduce the priest just for fun. He finally fell in love with her, but the affair resulted in their expulsion from the palace. The priest blamed her for their misery, angry with himself and with God for not saving him from his spiritual fall. He believed he was removed from his highest path, and that God should have saved him from losing the path of divinity. He felt lost, and that his fall was beyond repair.

The most beautiful part of this session was the Life Between Life—a profound message from the 'Source' was delivered. The myth of prayer and meditation, and the path back home was so beautifully described. Time stood still for as long as the message was being delivered; there was different energy enveloping everyone in the room, pin-drop silence and a kind of peace that one can only experience in an LBL session.

While delivering the message, the body language and the voice of the participant had changed; she spoke with such authority and conviction that it was awe-inspiring. It was a direct message from 'The Spirit.'

The participant spoke:

The best form of prayer is to praise my creation. Love this Universe and have compassion for any form of life, even the ones that seem dead to you. The best prayer is when in each word, thought and action of yours, you only have the highest good of all in mind. The best prayer is when you honour the life that has been bestowed upon you; it is when you feel the joy of life. The best prayer is when you allow love to guide you, to protect you and to lead you! The best prayer is when you have 'Gratitude' for all of your experiences, knowing you have been given the best. The best prayer is when you surrender in joy and embrace with 'Grace'! That's where the 'Bliss' happens. Prayer is not about locking yourself up in a cave and refusing life. That's your dogma, your stubborn ignorance. Where do you want to go with your prayers and mediation? I am right here, in this very moment, within you and within all that you hate. How can anyone take you away from me unless you are already away?. Love what you hate, and you shall see me.

The message continued as:
You carried such beautiful karma, that I gave you a palace, beautiful nature, luxuries, most sumptuous food of a king, and everything that would help you to live fully. Yet, not to have attachments; isn't that what you had asked for? Instead of enjoying what I gave you, you decided to choose suffering and hard discipline; never felt the joy. I sent a woman to experience true love, and you refused that too. How can you reach me if you do not feel the joy in any experience? The only way to me is through experiencing life fully, rejecting life is rejecting me. What prayer is that if it is taking you away from me?

Once the message was over, there was pindrop silence, and everyone wanted to soak in the energy, to grasp, and to imbibe this overwhelming, most earnest truth. Think about it for a moment, isn't it beautiful and doesn't it free you from your egocentric doer-ship?

That has been by far one of the most beautiful 'Life Between Life' sessions I have witnessed during a 'Soul Macrocosm Drama', the best prayer unfolding in front of us. The message was so clear because we were ready to receive it.

I am in awe of this Universe and how beautifully it orchestrates everything, makes sure you have the answers if you are curious enough to ask, and determined enough to know.

In the realm of source, the best prayer is to praise his creation. I feel so blessed to have witnessed such deep wisdom through my work, coming directly from the dimensions beyond, in a way that there is no chance of ever forgetting the lessons.

The simplicity and purity of this energy at work is so profound that it touches the very core of the soul, leaving an imprint impossible to erase. Creation's praise, gratitude and appreciation are your gateways to the heaven of Love, ease, joy and grace. THAT IS the only prayer.

***

6

Matter of Gratitude

The Root of Joy is Gratefulness

—David Steindl-Rast

Buddha has said: "Let us all stand up and be thankful, for if we did not learn a lot today, at least we learned a little, and if we didn't learn a little, at least we didn't get sick, and if we got sick, at least we didn't die; so, let us be thankful." Gratitude is our path to 'Bliss.' It is a craft that can turn anyone into an angel and any moment into magic. Gratitude can turn a stranger into a friend; it can make a house, a home. It can turn an experience into a lifetime memory. It is the beginning of a life of joy; it is an end to lifetime of anger, hate, trauma, and anguish.

Usually, when we are going through unpleasant situations, it is difficult to be grateful. During hard times, we are so consumed by one or more challenges at hand that we forget to see all the other hundreds and thousands of things that are happening perfectly.

The second principle of the 'Law of Attraction' says whatever you focus on grows stronger. When you focus on areas of your life that are bothersome, you attract more such tribulations. Remember, it is not what you desire, but how you feel, that signals the universe of your frequency, and then the universe gives you more of it. Gratitude prevents you from focusing on what you do not desire. It drives your attention towards the positive that is going on, causing you to feel good and blessed for all the things happening right. Your feelings then tell the universe—not only am I grateful, but these feelings of joy, bliss, and happiness are what I wish to have more of.

It is understandable to find it difficult to feel good and be grateful in situations such as losing a loved one, or when a close family member is critically ill, during a financial crisis or when a relationship is falling apart. But you must consciously make an effort and remind yourself that there is always a gift and brilliance in every situation. No matter how tough the going gets, it is yours and only yours to find the gift, learn the lesson, and make aware choices. Gratitude is a powerful tool that would never let you down. I have seen many miracles in my life since I started practicing gratitude. I saw the most complex relationships heal, finances improve, and much more. The case below is one that has always remained close to my heart.

In one of my first few 'Law of Attraction' workshops in Toronto, a gorgeous woman showed up. When I asked participants why they joined my class, she mentioned she was devastated by her marriage—her husband had been mistreating her—so she had come to find a way out of it. She felt catastrophic around him and dreaded his presence. She had come not to use the 'law of attraction' to mend the broken pieces but to use the information to ease her way out of her calamitous relationship. Her fear and agony were so intense that I wondered if he was some demon or something.

During the tea-break, she received a call from her husband;

she was visibly shivering, her hands shook, and she went pale. It took her a long mental preparation to answer the call. She had to gather the courage to hear him. I offered her a counselling session, and later she also did a past life regression to remove the root cause of her fear, so that she could deal with him in a calmer state of mind, where she could at least be comfortable while taking his call or when he would reach home from his office. I met her after a year—she was a different woman. She shared with me that her husband had changed too. They had even gone on a long holiday after almost a decade of their marriage. She told me the past life had cleared her fear, which was blinding her and did not allow her even to see the truth and then she mentioned something beautiful. She said, "Sahar, honestly, I did not understand much during the workshop as I was tense, his call had unsettled me completely; hence, I could not concentrate any more, but I understood gratitude. After my session, once the fear was gone, I practised it like a mantra, even though initially it felt fake. Slowly, I started to feel it, and that changed my relationship with my husband, and my relationship with my body." She had visibly lost weight and looked much more confident and radiant.

She had shifted her focus from all the ill-fate she believed she had encountered to all the blessings she had been showered with. She had started to notice and acknowledge what a great father and a skilled provider her husband was. She had started to thank the house, the body, the husband, his job, his boss, her home décor, her daughter. She said within forty days of her gratitude practice, she and her husband made love after seven years.

When I ask people to count their blessings, the list usually consists of friends, family, finances and sometimes briefly their body. We tend to overlook ourselves. What great blessings we are to ourselves and to this entire universe. We are here, so is the universe. Have you ever wondered what would happen to your universe, if you are not there? Your universe would cease to exist. Everything would go with you. My universe and your child's universe would remain, but yours would perish with you.

So, be thankful for your contribution. Have you been grateful to yourself for that beautiful heart you have been hiding? For the beauty you bring to your world? For the uniqueness of your body and your mind? For the way you have survived all that you have been through? For the DNA you carry? For the ancestors who gave you all that you needed to be who you are? For all the gifts and baggage they handed over to you, which has made you even more evolved? Have you been grateful to your mind which has protected you, helped you reach where you have? Have you thanked your parents not for just the support but also for all the complexities and shortcomings they have offered you so that you become the strong person you are today? Are you thankful to all your dreams, the ones that have been fulfilled and also the ones you had to let go because there was so much better stuff awaiting you? Have you been grateful to all those friends who left and rejected you, so that the new ones could come in and uplift you?

If you sit back and take an admiring look at your life, you will realise that there has not been a single moment which has not contributed to your growth at some level or the other. You may not be able to see or feel it as yet, but I assure you, you have only been progressing. At this moment, you are taking a leap of growth at all levels even though you may not know about it. You may be thinking—she is just vomiting some spiritual stuff. She has no idea what the hell is going on in my life. I agree with you, I know nothing about anyone's challenges, and I am not even saying they are easy to manage, but I certainly know how this universe functions. The fabric of this universe is of growth, and its currency joy.

Hence, you take one step towards changing your life, one thought towards growth, you speak one word of kindness, one phrase of appreciation, a willingness to do good, and the universe would push you a million steps ahead. It will gently and very gladly guide you, hold your hand and walk you through your mess till you see that you are the light in the tunnel and all this while there was no dark tunnel, but only that of your imagination. It would not only open innumerable doors of possibilities for you but also lead you every step of the way. Gratitude, however, is the master key. It has the secret code of the most protected vaults of abundance and grace.

We have been created in its essence, with the desire to experience and explore through the divine will, what can be more beautiful than being all that is?

I have hundreds of Gratitude stories to share. There is power in this simple practice, the kind of power that only 'the Source of all that is' possesses. The Creator is always in awe of its creation. He is in allowance of all that we do, all that we are and choose to be. He has no judgement and no complaints. That is the state of complete gratitude.

***

7

Compassion is an Inside Business

There is a nobility in compassion, a beauty in empathy, a grace in forgiveness.
—John Connolly

Quite late into my practice, I realised compassion was not what I thought it was. This term is used by most of us without really knowing its meaning. Everyone always talks about compassion and kindness; visionaries like Mother Teresa taught us by example, but not everyone is a visionary and most of us have not understood how to practice it. How do we use this word in our household? What is compassion, and how do we introduce this concept consciously into our daily life and spiritual practice?

The dictionary says compassion means to see, pity, understand another's suffering. Sometimes I wish there would be no language, as it has done the gravest damage to human consciousness. It has created the concept of culture, borders, manipulations, diplomacy and lies. Even though it is a great tool, yet it has been a very destructive one too. Through language, we've progressively lost touch with our authentic being. We have learnt to lie, hide the truth and rob each other of love, trust, honour and consciousness. I wish we could feel the words, instead of trying to understand them. It is through feelings that understanding becomes knowing, and knowing becomes wisdom. I wish for you to feel the knowing and not merely archive your understanding of some presented words. Let's decode compassion, as much as I have felt it.

For a long time, I felt compassion and kindness was about being nice and polite to people despite how they behaved; never saying or doing anything that would indicate in any way that I was upset with their words or behaviour. Never say no and never ever make anyone slightly uncomfortable. As therapists, we get even more disoriented, since there is a massive amount of information that is misunderstood, and most people only enact compassion and love; those who have become it are rarely seen. Like anyone else, I too was aping my environment initially. Talk to any healer or therapist, especially the ones who have been a few years into practice. They would all agree that at some point, they firmly believed that they were responsible for the whole world and felt it was their duty to heal everyone; reach out to everyone and offer help. I was no different.

Well, all the above is true, but this is a very tiny piece of compassion. It took me thirty-eight years—out of which ten had been of healing practice—to understand that to be a compassionate person means to have compassion first for my self. To be kind and patient with my self, to have my boundaries, to be assertive and be able to say 'No.' If we are not Mother Teresa, then being compassionate means to be able to hold the space for someone who is in pain, recognising and realising that they need to go through their journey because they have to learn their lessons. If we try and interfere more than what is required, we would only stop their experience, which would result in a reoccurrence of the lesson. Unfortunately, with every repetition, it only gets harsher. Compassion does not mean we try and help everyone just because we believe we know better (and maybe we do), or if we assume something is not good for a loved one, which may be a correct observation. Still, we cannot impose our opinion or interfere in their business, simply because that is not how the universe works.

It is also not about healing everyone, just because the role we are playing is of a therapist or a healer. Compassion is about being there; present with them, walking with them and understanding their pain without any judgement or sense of righteousness or superiority. We cannot be disappointed if they are not in a space where they can receive. A compassionate person would remain on standby until they are ready. He would offer to participate only in their truth and not their drama. Such a person would not entertain self-pity and victimhood. Compassion knows when to intervene and when to withdraw. It is to know and recognise our limitations and that of another, about setting up healthy boundaries and making sure not to overstep the border no matter how many needles we feel in our heart and not allowing anyone to cross our line too.

I remember the initial years of my practice, struggling with a few of my friends. I would get calls at 11 pm, 4 am and all through the day, for all kinds of healing. I remember the night I finally decided to put the nuisance to rest. I had a workshop that day starting early at 7 am. I had ten hours of class, followed by a magazine interview, after which a friend and his wife dropped by to seek some counselling for their marriage (even though I had politely told them that I wanted to rest after a long day). I was polite and thought they would understand but they didn't wish to. They stayed with me until 11 pm; I had to beg them to leave. That night as I fell asleep, I received a call from a friend saying she had a headache and needed healing, but that wasn't what made me understand the true meaning of compassion.

I received another call at 2 am from another friend; she asked me if I was sleeping, which of course required no answer, but what blew me off was that she went on to tell me she had had a vivid dream and could only think of me who could help her decode her dream. I could not believe what I was hearing. I was furious and amused at the same time. That was an indication for me that there was something majorly wrong with my sense of boundaries. I was inviting them to knock me off with my misconstrued interpretation of compassion. They were reflecting my lack of honour, nudging me to learn and have compassion for myself.

I learnt that compassion was to be there and know I would pitch in and help, but not at the cost of my truth. Not at the cost of my journey and not at the cost of me in any way. You can be truly compassionate with the world but not at your cost, compromising your truth, your plans, your dreams, and your passion; discounting yourself is not compassion, neither is sacrificing your life a noble act. They had to glorify such nonsense so that someone does the dirty job. It is merely a lack of self-worth; you need to find a way to work around it. Just be aware, there is a thin line between expressing compassion and imposing selfishness in the name of compassion. So how would you know which position are you operating from? To my understanding, the only way to know which side of the line you are standing is by knowing your intentions. Are you standing on the side of truth, the highest good of all, and your well-being at the same time? Or are you doing what you are doing

for settling scores or proving a point? Or in expectation of a
reward, ignoring the universe's gentle voice? Are you pleasing
people so that they will love, respect or appreciate you? Ask
your heart, it always has the answer.

***

8

Happiness Versus Joy

Joy is innate. Happiness is a practice.

I am fascinated by the word 'Happiness' in particular. When you look at human beings and interact with them, everyone wants to be happy while doing exactly the opposite of what can bring happiness. Interesting!

It is almost like a chase; everyone is running from pillar to post in pursuit of happiness. For some reason, man believes happiness is to be found, or maybe it is an achievement. There is another set of people who postulate happiness to be a state of mind. I feel both of them don't know what they are talking about. Happiness is not a state of mind; it is an emotion you experience through a faculty of the mind. It is the effect of a cause—one which is outside of you. It is physical in nature and dependable on an outside stimulus (precisely like anything else that is physical and dependent). There are the happy hormones secreted into our blood which cause us to be happy, as a result of a neurochemical stimulus in the body. The good news is that, like anything else that is physical, happiness too can be cultivated as a habit.

If you know a little about our physiology, you would know secretion of hormones is a result of mental or physical stimuli. That is why you can fake happiness by making changes in your physiology and environment; however, it would be transient. You feel happy in the company of people you love or when you receive a nice juicy compliment, achieve new goals, buy something new, travel or even when you shop, but they are all short-lived moments of a hormonal rush.

Joy, however, is of the soul. We are created with joy, out of joy, and to experience 'Joy.' Our innate nature is joy, hidden in a sacred, inner-most core of our being. We've quite successfully piled ourselves up with all kinds of stuff, so much so that we've lost our way to where joy resides, our own heart. Joy is what creation is composed of, and yet we are unable to reach it, we can't feel it. It is buried so deep that we have almost forgotten that we have it. Have you ever kept something valuable in a place so safe that you could find it no more? I have done that many times. We have done the same thing with joy. The mind is so scared of being happy that it chooses to hide it in the safest place possible, your own heart to which only you can have access, if only you would still remember the way. The only challenge is that even you can't recall why and where you have hidden your joy. We are so busy operating with our over-cautious, too fearful mind that we no more feel our heart; we can reach our soul no more. The mind is scared of being joyous simply because when there is joy, fear cannot exist.

We have learnt to fake happiness. As Abraham Hicks mentions, we can do activities that will keep us in the vortex for a longer period, but if it is not what we are, we will have dips sooner or later. With practice, you can increase its intensity and prolong the time you feel the happiness, but you won't be able to remain there endlessly, simply because you have no control over the mind during your sleep and many other times. If, as they presume, happiness is a state of mind, then you should not feel groggy if you have been practising it. The issue is you may try to be happy, but you are still trying.

Why try, if it is a state of mind? By that statement, we should be naturally happy. Everyone I have ever met, every single person has told me that to be happy and at peace is his ultimate goal. All that we do—work hard, earn money, name, fame and recognition; get married or exercise caution in choosing a companion, a profession; every announced/unannounced desire, chosen path and decision—all that is made with one motive and goal in mind—'Happiness'! A natural state of mind does not need so much effort. And if we are putting so much effort, then by now, we should have mastered it like any other practice. The hurdle is; we do not know the difference between happiness and joy. So what do we do?

First things first, we MUST stop the chase. The more you run after happiness, the less likely it is that you would find it, the more unhappy you would be.

The next step is to tap into joy and let go of desiring happiness. To tap into joy, you need to become a child again. A child has no worries; he does not wish to achieve anything; he doesn't care about others; he is so amused with himself that he is discovering something new all the time. He has no ego, doesn't take anything personally. He is an explorer, exploring his body and environment not for any achievement but for the sake of experiencing. He doesn't multi-task. If he is eating, then he is only eating, and then at a glance, his attention is focused on the new colourful toy, and then he stops eating because he wants the toy and then he hears the father's voice, he leaves the toy and runs to the father. He doesn't want to hold on to everything. He can let go easily and explore the next without being stuck in the previous. He is in the present, completely involved and engrossed with the new experience, everything else fades away to the background, and he doesn't care. No insecurities, no fear of losing or not having.

I remember my elder brother was famous for breaking every toy of his. He was an inquisitive child who wanted to know how his new toy—a bus—travelled from one place to another without a push. Or how the siren of the ambulance toy would produce the sound and the light. His childlike curiosity carries even today because he was allowed to remain a child. I, on the other hand, was made to grow up very fast. During my inner child sessions, I realised I have never lived as a child. I grew up way too quickly because at a very early age of 3, I was told (by actions of my mother and the words of my father) that my elder brother was unwell, and I was to take care of him. I was made the responsible child who had to make sure everything always happened right. By the time I was five-and-a-half years old, I had become a full-time mother upon the birth of my younger brother. When I compare the three of us, I see the difference: my elder brother, who was allowed to be a child by my parents was curious, more confident despite his speech issue. He is demanding like a child till now. He is the entitled one, whereas both my younger brother and I weren't allowed to remain children, we grew up with a sense of insecurity and uncertainty about ourselves. We were made responsible and with that came a fear of wrong-doing, of ever making a mistake. I had to get everything right because a sense of responsibility was instilled way too early. It has taken me years to learn to make an allowance for myself from a space of love and compassion, to accept that it's okay to make mistakes. I must confess, till a year ago, I did not know how to rest. I had to force myself to learn. This is how easily we discard, hide, and bury our inner child, the one who holds the key to joy.

Children don't need to impress anyone until we teach them otherwise. They have no fear. They would finger a power plug, run to hug any being from flowers and plants to animals and soft toys. They never wonder what if their ice cream finishes, how would the next one appear, or if the toy is broken, till we teach them not to share and not to explore. We scare them to tame them. We teach them with our fears and judgements using the same carrot-and-stick reward system. All the yap-yap I am doing is to gently remind you and then harshly hammer into you that the way to joy is past your ego. You need to drop it. Your self-image is what your ego is holding on to with all its might. The irony is no one perceives you and takes you as seriously as you do. King or pauper, whatever you think of yourself is your problem; no one else sees you as you think. If you choose to dissolve into the being of you, allowing the ego to beat its drum while you watch carefully, awareness would finally blossom. You continue doing all the stuff opposite of what the ego advises you to, and you would be close to recognising the joy. As you learn and continue to sweet-talk your ego-self to sleep, the authentic you awakens to a rise! A rise of joy, a sun that won't set as long as you choose awareness over ego.

Ego whispers into your ears that you must impress others. It mumbles in a rather compelling voice that you must oblige, please, adjust, compromise, follow, be a yes wo/man, adhere and be a part of the herd to be loved, accepted, approved and included. It cajoles you to dim your light so that you are respected, honoured and safe. Since the ego is completely disconnected from the soul-self, it can't fathom being aligned with the soul's plan and heart's desire. It is almost ossified with mania. Phobia of failing, failing in its own image. No one else takes you as seriously as your ego. It is a fallacy to believe you are as important to others as you expect yourself to be. It is crucial to inculcate the habit of coaching your mind, rather domesticate it, if you wish to be on the path of growth. It requires practice, perseverance and patience to unlearn and undo the mind's obsolete ways of existence, yet it is definitely worth the effort.

Once you befriend your ego-self and become your authentic self, you would then identify each time the ego would try to play you. Your chase for happiness and desperate need to be happy would be replaced with a sense of contentment, a sense of not only being enough but being whole and complete which is the dawn of your 'Inner Joy.' This discovery leads you to be the centre of your universe at all times. You would have a strong sense of a beautiful knowing—knowing that you are uniquely different— and that's how it is meant to be. The wisdom would be from a place of loving yourself and everything around you. It causes you to accept yourself for who you are, and your universe would respond to this union of you with your inner core by presenting to you all that which feels like magic. This allowance and acceptance, this ecstatic feeling of being in love with your existence, is what we call 'Joy.' You don't need any outside reason anymore; you are not only the joy itself, but also your cup is so full that it starts to overflow to all those around you.

***

9

Know Your Spiritual Powers

Using power is a sign of weakness, exploring your potential is, however, an exponential experience of creation.

Understanding the concept of 'Power' is as important as knowing love. If I ask you to close your eyes and repeat the word power for a couple of minutes, as you focus on your breath, you will sense a mild tension, a kind of excitement with an undercurrent of stiffness in your body and energy system. It is because power is a force used to do what seems difficult to do. You would never feel the need for power if you feel safe, secure, loved, and cared for. You only need it when an extra force is required to do what is not happening naturally for you.

In one of the 'Self Mastery' residential retreats I had attended, I felt like the teacher was preparing us for war. He kept on mentioning how dark forces will get after us during spiritual work, aiming to pull us down and eventually doom us. Before going for the retreat, I had a sense of discomfort. I told myself it maybe my resistance as it was a 'Self Mastery' course, and maybe my mind was not willing. When I reached the resort gate, a voice kept telling me something was wrong, and I must not go in. I almost took a U-turn, but my curiosity and thirst for learning took me past the gate. As my cab was entering the gates, I promised myself I would be very wary.

For the first two days of the workshop, it felt as if I had joined military training combined with FBI operations—to fight KGB spies and other invisible demonic forces searching for our angelic light, to blow it off. As he would start his fear-infusing statements, something inside my head would say, "Something is wrong, watch out!"

On the third day, some bizarre incidents started happening in our room. The window would open at night; dry fruits disappeared, candles blew a few times, which led me to investigate in my way (where I don't leave anything to chance and dig so deep that nothing can remain underground). I decided to follow the voice and get into my knowing and power (by power here, I mean trusting my knowing). I sat in meditation with a firm intention from a space of strength and not positive judgment or fear. It was then that I tapped into the voice and realised this gentleman was a tantric, creating fear in participants.

He was following the same old rule—make them fearful and helpless, and take charge of their energy system through the fear; make them so scared of this beautiful, loving universe that they shake and slowly lose themselves before every step. It was powerful learning and one that helped me save a dozen people from his intentions. I understood the difference between power-hungry spirituality and potential positive intentions. It was the beginning of tapping into my potential. I am so deeply grateful to the universe for wiring me the way I am; my mind does not surrender to fear. In my universe, I have only one cure for fear—to FACE IT head-on.

I am very thankful to this teacher, who honoured my soul contract and chose to play such a dark role to help me go beyond another layer of fear. That retreat was a divine intervention in my journey. It was divine guidance leading me and taking me into my fear of dark-work and right through it, guiding me to know different spheres of fear, albeit I had chosen a very unpleasant way of knowing.

It took me six-seven months to understand the multi-dimensions of fear and how it can affect our energy system. I went through a series of incidents that would put any Hollywood horror movie scriptwriter to shame. I came face-to-face with the challenges of the unknown, energies powerful enough to cause a crack in my bedroom wall. But I had decided to stand in my power, determined to unfold many facets of myself which I was unaware of; I stood my ground. I was a warrior, and defeat had no place in my dictionary. I would not give up; I would not give in and would fight it till the end. Those seven months led me to the most powerful knowing, and that is—we do not need power; the greatest power is that of love, wisdom, good intentions and faith.

Why would anyone need power? Power is required to get things done forcefully, to destruct and to control. To evolve spiritually, you do not need spiritual, or any form of power, all that you need is to tap into your potential. Power is used to either defend or attack. Who are we attacking, and what are we protecting against? It is always us versus us. I wonder if you need power to either attack yourself or defend yourself from you—doesn't it sound insane?

To go beyond you, you need will-power, not power. Spiritual is your innate state of being; there is no scope to become more spiritual. You need will-power to tap into your potency which is of 'love and joy.'

The spiritual world is simple. You stay in your business, go after your truth, clean your mess, and everything else is simply what you have invited either as a mirror, reflection or a projection or simply because you believed in it and just had to experience it. There is nothing more to it.

Many people, including myself, would have had encounters with people and energies which did not feel light. They may even have felt scary, demonic, notorious, and some persistently misleading and misbehaving. All that you need to remember is that everything within your experience, within the objective physical realm or the subjective spiritual domain, is a result of your questions and your curiosity. Believe it or not, your imagination and what you have been seeking brings you all the experiences. They rightly say—what you seek is seeking you.

So seek love, joy, ease and grace.

Those who seek power in any form are eventually drawn to it. If you wish to fly, all that you need is to recognise who you truly are. The only war you need to fight is the war with your ego, which is causing you fears and insecurities. Eliminate your self-doubt, your need for approval and all the challenges you have put up against you. In this battlefield, your only weapon is 'Love.' Love towards who you are, ever have been and ever will be, including your dark shadows, your body and your mind.

***

10

Positive, Negative and the Dark

With all certainty, after an extremely turbulent and difficult life, I can affirm that nothing in this existence is ever negative. I am talking not in terms of physics, but in terms of creation. Nothing that's created can ever be negative or bad, not even lizards, which I still have a phobia of. Most people I meet, at some point during our association, ask me if there is anything negative, creating obstacles in their life, or if someone has used some dark practice on them. I feel sad that a human being who is the most-evolved creation feels so helpless, even though I understand that this feeling of powerlessness has been with man for all of his existence. My answer to this question is what my mother taught me when I was eleven.

Mahboobeh, my mother's friend, knew coffee cup reading, a tradition in the Middle East. Once in a while, when friends got together, they would ask Mahboobeh joon (dear) to see their future in the aromatic Turkish coffee residues. The whole culture and mystery behind it was so fascinating to me that I would make sure not only my homework but both my brothers' homework was done by the time the house filled with the aroma of coffee. I would then be sitting next to Mahboobeh joon with all my senses on high alert. I remember once she had a very worrying expression when she read the coffee imprints for a lady whose cup she was peeping into. She said someone in the family had done black magic and that it would cause health issues to her son. There was tension in the air; questions were thrown back and forth. The fun activity suddenly had everybody feeling very uneasy.

After everyone had left, I asked my mother—what was black magic? My mother explained that some people who don't love themselves, sometimes forget how to be good. They do things that would harm others. I asked her, would Amir (my playmate and son of the other lady), be affected? I remember my mother, a very gentle woman otherwise, held my shoulders and looked into my eyes, her gaze piercing. She said, "Listen Sahar, my child, if you believe in black magic, it will affect you, and if you don't believe in it, it can never affect you! Remember that." That gaze, her hands on my shoulder and her firm voice made a very long-lasting impression on me. It is what I believe even today and pass on to my clients.

Let me talk about the negative a bit. Once this is clear, then you would know the positive too. There are five truths you must inhale into your lungs and allow them to be taken to every cell in your body through your blood. These are essential principles for a life of ease, joy and grace.

Truth 1: There is absolutely nothing 'Negative.' The only negative is the electron in an atom, and you realise it is quite harmless. There might be stuff you don't understand or do not know about, which may feel scary, but that does not make it negative; it is only unknown to you.

Truth 2: Energy is the base of everything. Energy is neither positive nor negative. It brings us to the fact that nothing can be negative in its essence.

Truth 3: 'Negative' in real terms usually refers to that which is not working for you. In other words, 'Negative' is a frequency of energy that is not in harmony with yours. Hence, it feels uncomfortable, heavy, and when unknown, maybe even scary.

Truth 4: Anything that is seemingly negative to you is a result of your powerful ability to create that incident, challenge a situation to experience and overcome it. Since it is your creation, you have the power and the choice to change it, replace it with what feels good to you.

Truth 5: 'Negative' is simply a message from the universe, trying to tell you it is time you change and replace what has crossed its expiry date. To drop what needs to go or heal what is causing you disalignment with your path. It is the universe telling you to realign.

Pretty much everything else is positive, including the negative, if we understand the 'Grand Overall Design.'

***

11

Myths of Healing and Therapy

Perhaps you are reading this book because you have started healing yourself. Maybe you are a healer, and you are seeking more clarity in response to your calling. What matters is that you are on the way. It is not so important where in the journey you have reached, what is commendable is that you are taking one step at a time. On this path, it is vital to know about healing and helping. What to heal and how? Who to help and receive help from? One of the most confused states any traveller on this journey would go through is of the extent of help they can offer and from whom they should seek guidance. Most of the times, people are befooled, taken advantage of, and usually, their boundaries are compromised.

Healing comes from the English root 'haelen', meaning to cure, save, make whole. You cure that which is not healthy, and you make whole that which you know whole of. The question is, who can you make whole? Well, not so difficult to reply to that one—the answer is 'Only You.' You can't make anyone else whole and complete, simply because you do not know the whole of anyone else; hence it is impossible to make them whole and complete without their conscious, active, participation.

If you are determined enough and also have been chosen, at the maximum what you can do is to know yourself completely. That we call Buddhahood, and no Buddha ever wanted to heal others. Till then, we will keep trying to help others while our wounds are still bleeding, and the reason is clear, our ego operates from 'Doing.'

You must heal yourself to a great extent before you attempt to heal/help anyone else. It is also essential to know your boundaries while healing or helping others. You can heal those who truly wish to heal; you can't help those who are unwilling to receive.

Like all other practitioners of energy work, I too have gone through all these phases of wanting to reach out, giving unsolicited advice, offering to help, losing sleep over other's challenges, et al., but I realised that was my ego. I completely understand when you want to save the whole world and heal everyone who is in any form of discomfort; I've been there too, but that's a camouflage that the ego is using. No one is the 'Messiah of the World', and it is not your job to heal everyone. The only piece of life you are responsible for is YOU. All that you need to do is to focus on your healing, and in return, everything else would start to fall in place.

If at all, you are guided to heal and help because you believe that is your life's purpose, then you must first heal yourself.

Similarly, helping others needs to be done in balance. Helping others does not mean that you allow others to take advantage of you; in fact, I believe there is no need to help anyone. You can guide them, teach them and empower them, but eventually, they need to take care of their stuff. No one is helpless, they may feel helpless, but everyone is powerful beyond measure. No one needs help, just a bit of clearing the fog so that they can see how powerful they are. People can be tired, weak or lost, but never helpless. Everyone has the same source, same energy, same God/ Universe; they can be just facilitated to find the way but walk, they must.

If you are choosing this path as your life purpose, you need an extra dose of awareness. It is critical to be reminded at all times that every intention, thought, word and action put this powerful energy that is the source of everything into motion, which creates an energy attachment, an entanglement. It is extremely crucial to be aware of the kinds of entanglements we create. Violation of other's space, imposing of any form, getting into other's business even if it is for the sake of helping and healing, can have karmic consequences that we won't be pleased to know about.

You don't want to get entangled in another person's karma. You have enough of yours to handle. It is not so difficult to know if you are getting off track. You have to watch yourself and what is going on in your head, despite your actions. If you are making others dependent on your help and healing, you are not healing or helping; you are practising control in a whole new soap opera. If you feel a sense of ego and pride, and think you have saved anyone or that only you could do that or what a great deed you have done; if you are the doer, then you are operating from ego. If you are healing/helping for any tangible or intangible rewards, award or recognition, if you feel bad for those you stood by and were available to are no more in touch or don't acknowledge your contribution, you are operating from ego.

You know when you operate from an I-Know-It-All or Thou-Shalt-Save-the-World attitude.

You enter the scene as a helper/healer/contributor when asked, do as much as requested, and exit as nobody, as soon as the work is done, without attachment to the result, or need to know the outcome nor any expectations of reward. Any of the missing ingredients above and you are getting into something that's so not your business.

It is pertinent to your spiritual health that at every step you take a pause and ask yourself—why am I doing this? How am I feeling about what I am doing? What is it that I am expecting as a result of this act? At any point, if you detect doer-ship, you need to stop and heal your self.

***

12

Sex and Spirituality

Sex has always been a topic of great importance and ignorance at the same time. Sex is an act through which the extreme ends of polarity come closest to each other and lose themselves in allowance of their differences for the higher purpose of creating life—a precise manifestation of creation by the 'Creator.' The fact that the feminine and the masculine genders come together, and merge into oneness is the most beautiful, divine magic of creation. Today sex has been merely reduced to the meeting of two bodies, whereas, it is the most blessed phenomena, a soft, delicate play for us to witness and feel the beauty, the love, the passion and oneness of the process of creation, as the source's generous progeny.

In the physical realm, sex would have been closest to how the Creator feels while breathing his creation into existence. When two souls touch the deepest core of each other to become one and step into the magnificence of the Creator's only purpose: 'Expansion of this existence.' However, here too, man has failed to touch the essence. He has reduced the most majestically sacred process of creation to merely a bodily pleasure, a profane and not even that—he has turned it to the most abused act ever.

Intimacy is supposed to be an act of compassion and tenderness; an enthralling experience of passion and warmth. A desirous, and yet freeing, encounter of man and his Creator. Sadly, the collective consciousness has been messed up, and the 'Universal Law of Gender' has been abused; man has been manipulated, losing the sacredness of it all.

'Law of Gender', a mighty 'Universal Law' which has been very conveniently removed from most old, religious and new-age spiritual books, is a topic worth knowing about.

The law of gender indicates that everything in nature and this universe has a 'Masculine' and 'Feminine' aspect to it and that everything has a gestation period to actualise. Wherever you look at in nature, you see both feminine and masculine aspects at play. Be it plants or animals or any other form; it takes both to procreate in this universe. According to Kybalion, gender is everything; it embodies the truth that there is gender manifested in everything.

There is not one aspect of life where the masculine and feminine principles are not at work. It is true on all three planes— the 'Physical Plane', the 'Mental Plane' and the 'Spiritual Plane.'

On the 'Physical Plane', this manifests as sex, on the higher planes it takes higher forms, but the principle remains the same. Creation can't take place on the physical, mental or spiritual planes without this law.

Everything has a yin and yang. On the physical plane, each person has a male or female physical body; however, psychologically each person is androgynous with male and female qualities. Without the dual principle of male and female, there could not be a difference of potential, the perpetuation of motion, nor regeneration.

I think I have said enough to give you a hint that two feminine principles can't procreate and that is against the universal law. However, with the movements that are taking place, we are told otherwise, and now people are fighting for it. Everyone is free to feel how they wish to feel, and perhaps that is another experience, another level of evolution.

There is no possibility of any phenomena without reason behind it. However, it may be possible that we have to experience the polarity of creation to finally choose what is pro it and what is against it. Suppose we look at it from the 'Source' level of awareness and planning. In that case, there is no possibility of creation going wrong in deciding the 'Gender' of the next life as the 'Creator' is undoubtedly accurate and precise. These universal laws are in place to make sure there is zero error in maintaining balance, order, and continuous cycle of creation and expansion.

From all my experiential cases of people who lack understanding of their gender or are confused about it, there is one evident thing. And that is—through a loving-caring course correction therapy, they can get in touch with who they are, and be grateful for how the Creator has created them. Like many other conflicting realities, this has been a seed planted into human consciousness long ago. Perhaps that is the reason why almost no book talks about the 'Law of Gender' in a way that would bring clarity. Unless these two principles come together and remain balanced in all planes of existence, we would not be aligned with our plan and the universal design. There's no denying that whatever is happening is always right.

I do not know why this experience has been introduced to human consciousness; it's my prayer that the learning is complete, and balance is restored.

Another important universal law is the 'Law of Balance.' If

you have a close look at nature, you realise that when there is balance, there is vitality and growth. Whenever there is an extreme imbalance, nature has to create balance through some natural calamities. Similarly, any form of growth can happen only in the fields where balance is maintained. Today we live in a world where everything has become about extremes. Everything is happening at extremes; it almost feels that we are facing a pandemic of obsessive-compulsive disorder. People are getting obsessed with and addicted to clean eating, vegetarianism, minimalism, materialism, pornography, sex, substance, anti-ageing, the colour of their skin and even meditation (the list is long).

In spirituality too, we have people leaving home and family, renouncing the world, opting for extreme practices and food habits, desiring to achieve something that does not exist. A side of spirituality refers to sex as a means of rising of wild, powerful feminine energy—Shakti—and attaining Kundalini awakening. Some practices use sex for heightening the spiritual experiences, awareness and increasing the spiritual power, and even improving mental faculties.

Some forbid any form of intimacy and think sex, love and intimacy are evil and a hindrance to the soul's evolution. This category appears rather strange to me. I wonder why the Creator would create us the way it has. Do these people think that the 'Source' was sitting idle and decided instead of throwing it away, let me for the fun of it, install it in human beings and all of animal consciousness, and then upon adding those to us, he looked at us and thought, 'sex organs look good on them!' Could there be anything the source would have created without a purpose? Who are we to deny the process of creation?

Or did the source think—let me hide the secret to moksha

and the universe in their genitals. And then the Tantric discovered that it is through sex they can reach moksha or some heightened spiritual level of awareness.

I do not deny people may have awakened their kundalini through tantra sex. Neither do I deny that some saints may have had the most beautiful oneness experiences as a result of their practice of celibacy, but these are not the only ways, and they do not have to be. There is no evidence that anyone has attained enlightenment or salvation through any of the practices of extreme harshness. There would be a billion ways of being spiritual, knowing the self, falling in love with the Creator and being one with the source. The point is what works for you, whatever that may be; you need to stick to it, keeping the structure of the universe, your journey and the universal laws in mind.

Sex is fantasised, and at the same time, it is a taboo. Something that man has chosen to explore behind closed doors to the extent of extreme abuse and addiction. He feels pride in his many explorations in his twisted mind, but he has chosen not to talk about it because being authentic about it is a sin. That is quite ludicrous; we lie to ourselves and each other, resisting the process of creation, making it a shameful act and creating more shameful acts around it, and yet we can't talk about it to resolve it. The point we are missing here is that morality has nothing to do with the act of sex.

To understand this sacred means of procreation and co-creation, we must first separate the morality from it. This process is a gift to mankind by an infinite superintelligence. Its ambitious vision of expanding creation is facilitated through our bodies. It is when the two physical bodies come together, all other bodies merge and entangle with each other. At that moment, both poles of gender and the entire polarity, experience love, passion and oneness, which could be the closest to how the Creator feels while creating this universe. When two bodies meet, their souls have already met. They have found each other and have got together for a reason—if the reason is union, the relationship turns out to be of love, harmony and mutual growth. If the reason for this meeting is of unfinished business, revenge and writing off scores of any kind, it can lead to abuse, rape or any unpleasant and undesirable experience.

It is during sex that two souls come closest to each other—their occupied bodies, life juices, energy bodies, chakras, memories of the past come together. They overlap each other, mixing and merging and becoming one at a point and then screaming—maybe even silently—in that ecstasy of oneness. They lose oneself into another with no inhibition whatsoever, experiencing that moment of absolute joy, passion and pleasure, excitement and calmness, all at the same time. Where nothing else matters and from that point of union in love, creation of another life takes place. Isn't it supposed to be beautiful?

Orgasm would have been closest for human beings to be able to feel the joy the Creator feels, as he creates this universe! But we have made that mechanical too. We plan the exact time and date, even body position. I wonder when did we lose the being in us and became the 'doing' in every aspect of life.

Like anything else, both categories of people—those who change partners like dirty clothes, and those who deny themselves the experience of intimacy to reach heightened levels of spiritual practices or source—haven't been able to rise beyond the basic levels of physicality or greed for spiritual power. They are missing the whole point of this most beautiful prodigy of existence called 'Earth-life.' Both are stuck in ignorance, one at the physical level and the other at the spiritual level.

How can anyone become one with the Creator while abusing or denying a part of source's creation and by repulsing the very process of it?

The whole game of self-realisation is about 'Awareness' and 'Balance.' Changing too many partners too often, and being intimate with anyone without a deep sense of connection, is not advisable. You would be allowing people with all their baggage, entanglements to enter your space and connect with you in the most karmically inter-twisted manner. To leave their energy imprints and unauthorised energy connections within you and your life while you would be lending a piece of you to them. The more the encounters, the more scattered you would be.

If you are not doing what you are doing with an aware choice, it is most likely that with each intimate relationship, no matter how good the sex felt, you start feeling less of yourself. Feeling more bruised, both mentally and emotionally, and less worthy of your authentic self. And to cover that void, you would have another encounter and the vicious cycle continues till one day you would be knocked off. The more this imbalance happens, the less likely you would be to meet your 'Divine Life Partner.' The imprints left on you would make it difficult for the other soul to recognise you. You too would have difficulty trusting your knowing and would not be able to differentiate and acknowledge the connection or reciprocate. By then you would have been entangled enough not to recognise your true self, how can anyone else recognise you amidst all those energy imprints?

It usually takes about eight years to completely clean your system of energy imprints if you are making moderately diligent efforts at healing yourself. You can do the maths yourself.

Sometimes the feelings and excitement about a person is powerful, which can mislead you completely. Before you jump into any conclusions about your new-found love and just before you zero-down on the person being your soulmate/twin flame—just because you consulted Google to feel good about your feelings—pause!

If you cannot figure out what is happening and why all your feelings and hormones are all over the place, consult a therapist or a guide, you would save yourself many post-break-up sessions and loads of money. My approach to life and every aspect of it is realistic; I honestly believe ignorance is NOT bliss and neither an excuse. I would rather know the bitter truth and heal it than closing my eyes and staying in the cocoon of my blissful ignorance. I have no judgement and charge attached to anything; life has taught me that not all that sparkles is gold. At the same time, I firmly believe every uncut, unpolished diamond has the chance of being a royal jewel, only if you choose to go through the heat and the tedious process.

I suggest whenever in confusion, consult someone who can guide you without any biases. Never be in a hurry; centre yourself, take a break, breathe and follow your awareness to avoid empty, toxic entanglements. I suggest you be intimate with awareness, not because someone has a hot body, tons of money or has swept you off your feet with a creative mind. Appreciate all, but you don't have to complicate your energy for any of those. Don't rush into a relationship because you can no more take the loneliness.

Take your time and move in or out of relationships with awareness. I have had relationships/friendships which were out of compulsion, an escape from loneliness and difficult times. These associations left me extremely bruised and guilty. It took me a decade to recover, and I don't wish the same for you.

***

Book Four
From Awakening to Self-Realisation

1

Uncover Your Beautiful Self

The only purpose of your birth is to awaken to your truth. To reach the deep, blissful, joyous Godliness that you truly are. I don't care how much of dirt, mud, fungus or whatever else you have piled up inside of you, I know deep inside, your very essence is that of joy, peace, bliss and compassion. It is your job to uncover your beautiful, magnificent self. This process of finding yourself is what the entire search is all about. Find yourself right where you are.

There are different and sometimes not-so-easy phases during your spiritual quest. The spiritual journey is like the snakes and ladders game; you keep moving up and down, back and forth, biting yourself and picking yourself up time and again. It can be tiring, it would feel lonely, and many a time you would wish if you could go back to the ignorance stage, as it seems like a never-ending game and quite a Spartan place to be in when the biting happens too often. Yet you would keep on moving because deep inside you know there is no going back, the only way out is to keep moving inwards. Since you are on the path to enlightenment, here is another truth to learn. You do not have a free will here, once the dreamer has dreamt you into existence, you are only going to evolve; the only difference is that till some stage you would not be aware of it. The moment the call has been made, and you have asked those golden questions, you are put into a washing machine, which you only knew how to turn on; it will be turned off as per his will and not yours.

You may have been drugged to believe otherwise; many free-will slogans are being screamed, but as they say, half knowledge is more dangerous than none at all. The understanding of how free-will works is very shallow; the extent of free will has not been discussed in detail. Your awakening is like you admitting yourself in a rehab centre, where you are the drug, the antidote, the rehab centre, the doctor and even the counsellor. You go through similar stages as a substance addict would go through during his cleansing process. The day you get over the bone-crushing pain of letting go of ignorance and let in your knowing about the delusional mind, that's the day of your awakening. You enter this place when you start questioning your existence. And then the nightmare begins, you would go through all the withdrawal symptoms, the hallucinations, physical, mental and emotional pain; the disbelief in your ability that you can remain clean and walk the path. Once you overcome these aspects, it becomes an adventure where you are jumping cliffs on a free fall, knowing you would be held or learn to fly.

The process is addictive, both for genuine seekers and the by-passers. There is as much intensity in the force that is guiding you forward, as in you resisting the path. The resistance is of your mind that wishes to inhale one puff of Maya to go back to the world that is built on pain. The mind is numb to it like an addict is to his dose of morphine, the last stage is when you realise you are in it for good. That this is an eternity term you would serve. You then surrender out of having no choice and not out of your free will. The surrender brings in the other side of human consciousness into play, now that the reptilian brain has failed in attempting both fight and flight strategy, the result-oriented, problem-solving aspect of you kicks in, and the learning process starts. Slowly you get the hang of it and begin to enjoy the new way of 'Being.' To remain here and move forward from this point, you need to be strong-willed. You are to avoid old company, anyone/anything that may pull you back into your old frequency. Perhaps you need to change your contact number—that is your energy frequency—so the lower ones can't match you.

You are asked to follow a healthy lifestyle to make sure you stay healthy and clean, maybe meditate, eat clean and pump all those muscles that would help you pave the way forward and feel good about who you are becoming while you keep remembering the dark place you have emerged from. It's important to remember everything, the pain you had been through, and the pain you caused others, the 'Old karma.' Once this stage is over, a beautiful shift takes place, and you start finding joy even in incidents that may feel uncomfortable. You would find a reason for all the delays. You begin experiencing a new level of patience with all the hard work you put in, and you move from result-hungry to process-geek. Everything starts to feel smoother and look brighter. Old concepts find new meaning and no matter how hard you try to feel your old self, you realise the new you is softer yet firmer, more compassionate and less worrying. You see through stuff, and yet nothing bothers you. The knowing that was painful in the earlier phases is now the source of your peace and bliss. You are now self-realised, moved from an awakened you to a 'Self-Realised' you where you have seen many shades of you and accepted that the greys too were created by you. After all, grey too is a colour.

Each phase and how long you stay there would depend on what your journey is all about, how much more are you willing to work on yourself. What would the Creator have planned for you? Once you are comfortable with why you are here, you set your ships sailing once again. This time you have a different mission, you realise the real you is of limitless potency; you leave the shore in search of your higher SELF, leaving the self behind and you become the 'I Am.'

From 'Awakening to Self-Realisation' is like having a boat on a small artificial lake, it may get a bit tough but is quite manageable. It is from self-realisation to being 'Realised' that your skills are put to test. Time and again, you will come face-to-face with death as you go through the storms of the ego; this is the death of all images of yourself you once held real. You will have to survive high tides of denial, receding waves of resistance, tsunamis of confusion and exhaustion from the sail. It is surely not an easy sail, but it is all worth it. You can't stop at being 'Self Realised.' If you have managed to reach here, something inside you will push you forward. You have taken a path very few would dare step on, and the universe won't let you stop. Once at this junction, you would be itching for more; your soul would be aching to set itself free. By now, your mind too realises that a gigantic, prodigious intelligence has taken over, and is running the show.

As mentioned in earlier chapters, everything in this universe is always fighting for survival—so is your mind. It will put up a great fight, but with less strength. If you remain prudent, you realise that it gives up much more easily, and your knowing curve moves much faster. Of course, we can't let the mind die; it has the key, and without the mind, even this existence would not have been possible. So you need to nurture it while you keep reminding your mind that you are the 'Master' now.

Everyone goes through similar stages, only the coping mechanism is different. The voyage is lonely, a bit scary and exhaustive, but at the same time, it is beautiful, mesmerising and rewarding. The reward is the treasure called YOU.

You move from the limited ego-self to the infinite loving soul. When you walk the path, at some point, you reach a tiny bridge, where the self is prohibited from crossing, you can't walk together anymore. You have to drop the self upon which you become the path itself. You and the journey become one. You now have entered the land of 'Love and Bliss.' Like everything else, nothing is permanent; you may remain there or keep going back and forth, but, as they say, practice makes you perfect. Once you master being in that state, you realise a growing sense of awareness, slowly the desire to reach the destination dissolves, as you have become the destination. You then know there is nowhere to go, nothing to do or attain, nothing to achieve but to drop everything and let go.

Remember this adventurous tour is not of achieving and doing, but of releasing, re-discovering and becoming. There would be sleepless nights of stomach-wrenching emptiness, nauseated void of old you, painful migraines of confusion and disbelief, heart-aching loneliness, but there is undoubtedly light. The light is not at the end of the tunnel, but the light is you in the tunnel. It's just that you have been put into hypnosis for aeons of time—with your eyes closed, and your mind programmed to keep the blindfolds on—you just believed in the story of the dark tunnel. Take those blindfolds off, count yourself out of the hypnosis, open your eyes and desire to SEE CLEARLY and you shall only see the light and feel 'Only Love.'

One day you would drop the need to walk any path. The day you surrender to your inner wisdom, you know all that you need to do is to drop old baggage, as you don't need to pack for anywhere but to be 'soul-naked'; you become the destination, detached from any expectation, of any reward or results. You let go of all attachments, even your devotion to truth. A deep sense of faith would take you to the place of least resistance and the meadow of all-knowing. As you step on the green grass of truth, the warm rays of love would fill your entire being. It is the light of love that melts your inner self and the outer shadow into one existence. You become one with all of you. You allow the innermost essence, that beauty of your unique soul signature, to slowly penetrate to your entire being, overflowing to all of that which is your existence, realigning the universe that you had believed, into the one that really 'Is.'

The entire universe would feel one. You are centred and connected to your very being, in total allowance of your essence, hence allowing and accepting others to be who they are. You operate from complete acceptance as you know that is the state in which judgements drop, fears fade, love prevails, and grace overtakes.

The 'Realised You' recognises you in everyone and every situation around you, it honours the source and its choice of creation in everyone and everything. A deep sense of gratitude replaces insecurities and nothing but your feeling of goodness matters. The 'Realised You' rejects everything disharmonious, not from a sense of judgement, but from a space of self-love and compassion for all those involved. It would realign with that which is only love, knowing that everyone is surely an expression of divine consciousness and yet some may choose to take more time to express the divinity within them; that is perfectly okay like everything else always is.

***

2

Father of All Spiritual Myths: Moksha

The invisible, sugar-coated 'Golden Carrot'—that's the ultimate aim of all human beings. To attain salvation is what every spiritual practice believes and aims at; I too wasted a good portion of my practice on the same (though I say wasted, perhaps it is important for everyone to go through the same process). Let's break this down. Even though the word salvation has been referred to in many complicated ways in the Bible and all other scriptures, I will attempt to explain it in a simple language. (I often wonder what was the purpose of saying anything at all, if they said stuff making sure either we didn't understand it or understood the opposite of it.)

So let's understand the basics. Salvation in the English dictionary is mentioned as 'a means of escape specifically from sins, preservation from sins.' At some places in the Old Testament, it is a simple, concrete relation between man and God. The word 'Moksha' is used in Buddhism, Hinduism, and Jainism, and has its root in the Sanskrit word 'muc' which means to release, let go, and liberate. Basically, by salvation, we mean to free ourselves from our sins and let go of our guilt and shame. How did we conclude that salvation meant to go somewhere? Is it not better to work on not committing a sin than to say a complete NO to life and wanting to escape the wheel of life to avoid sin?

If moksha is about man's relationship with his God, let the man find his God. Who is anyone to tell him how his relationship with his God should be and who knows how everyone's God is, to suggest a sure-shot remedy of healing the strained relationship of every man with his God?

If we go by the liberation aspect of it, I feel being on earth is where man is most liberated, going into the literal meaning of liberation. As soon as Adam had the apple, God said, you now do whatever you want; you are too impure a being to be with me. Seriously? What kind of God is that? Where did all his love and compassion go? Just for an apple? It's only on earth that so much is happening; look at all the realms of 'Angels and Masters', no sin is being committed there, so I believe this is the ultimate freedom, where man is doing what he wants, and getting away from it, life after life. Someone has to ask these moksha-promising Gurus that when there is no sin in the realm of angels and masters, why aren't they still liberated?

No one bothered to explain that eating the apple symbolises going against the 'Divine Will' which means you have no free will when it comes to how this universe operates. The apple represents the mind—the mind that makes you wander. The snake is the reptilian aspect of our mind, one that has all the tools of survival up its sleeve. The wise one—Eve—symbolises the expression of life! You can only express the life that the source has created through your unique perception, as you keep on creating your own unique experiences.

All the stories of liberation, salvation and ascending are

myths, and I am determined to bust this myth for you. Knowing the truth and making aware choices is true empowerment. You may still go ahead and sin, and then find a Guru to clear your sins, but then that would be an aware choice. If we go by the cyclic motion of life while we remember that the source is in everything and everything is within the source, then my question is: where would we go after being liberated? Back to the source, isn't it? But isn't the source in everything, and hence we would be back into everything? This tall claim of moksha does not make any sense no matter how many times I try to fool myself!

Let's revise once for the benefit of being on the same page. First, you were punished and sent here; then you were told the best way to finish this suffering is by improving your relationship with an entity outside of you called God, and then they said that you must escape from where God sent you so that you sin no more. Isn't it insane? Would your all-knowing, all-forgiving and all-loving God do that to you? They also tell you—you will then go somewhere, where either seventy-two virgins are awaiting you or somewhere where you would burn in flames of fire. You sinned by having an apple—why didn't God send you straight away to the fire? Is earth your bail period, or does God need so much time to decide the quantum of your punishment? I thought He was very efficient, and here He is, behaving like the judiciary in India, taking forever to decide.

Well, none of the above makes sense, because it is not the truth. It is not false either; the only challenge is that for some reason whoever came up with these stories seems to be a sadist, who enjoys making humankind more confused and watches them running after their tail like a dog. If someone wanted to help humanity, then he should have used simple language.

This one lie has caused more sins than any other ever. It has put man on fire, with a sense of competition to see who reaches God first. Some out of 'ignorance-originated good-will', and others out of 'ignorance-generated greed', have done extensive damage to human consciousness that it looks beyond repair to this day.

The other school, which is spirituality, talks about moksha as freedom; when the soul frees itself from all the activities of earth and ascends. It moves beyond the cycle of karma and becomes free of cause and effect. It joins its Source/Creator back.

One of man's challenges, as well as gifts, is that he is very impatient and loves to conclude. He refuses to believe that he may not know it all. Man loves to believe that he has an answer to every question. It is so naïve. We have not even understood our own body completely, yet we are continuously concluding theories about the universe. If we did have all the answers, we should have been disease-free and yet we think we have answers to the questions of the soul.

I wonder if those who came before us did not know or they purposefully kept the truth from us; there is evidence that makes me feel and believe that while they may not have lied, they haven't told us everything they knew either. Why would they talk the same language and yet deny each other, and never bother to correct what the other had not said? Something seems amiss. And then there are spiritual practices that promise you salvation. Self-acclaimed Gurus who tell you their way would free you. My suggestion is if you ever find such a Guru, run away or just for the sake of fun ask him—if that is so, then what is he doing here when he has figured it all out? A real Guru will give you hints and prompt you to find your way. Those who know it all are the ones you need to be wary of.

I had a domestic help named Geeta. We had a firm bond; she was not only my housekeeper but also my messenger; wise indeed and a clairvoyant, evidently an old soul. In many of my talks, I would give her example saying—we must not judge anyone based on their circumstances today, for all that I know maybe my help Geeta would have been my Guru of the past.

After a few years of working with me, one day, she asked me to take her into a past life session. She said she wanted to know a few things and also what was her connection with me. When she went into a trance, she entered a past life where he (she was a male in that lifetime) was a Guru in India, with a following of about 5,000 people from the nearby villages. I was his very devoted disciple. What she saw next was great learning for me. He had promised everyone salvation, due to which his followers were very devoted to him. She then moved to the last day of that life and saw himself on the death-bed, confessing to me at that moment that he had been lying, that he knew nothing about salvation. I was comforting him by telling him that I knew all along that he didn't know. As his disciple, in that life, even though I knew everything, but my reverence and honour for him were greater than his lies, so I forgave him. I promised him that when we met next, I would help his soul remember all his lessons. (Geeta being my help everywhere, had attended more than 300 of my workshops and even participated in nearly 30 'Family Constellations.')

In that session, when I moved her to 'Life Between Life', the Masters spoke a great message through her. Her guides told her that she had chosen to serve me, as I would help her soul in seeking the truth and the truth was salvation CAN-NOT be learnt or attained; only the source grants it. It is what the soul would have chosen, and it cannot be learnt; it can only happen through the self by the source. One of her guides then went on to elaborate: "When the soul is ready, when lessons are learnt, and remembered, when all becomes one and one becomes free of the 'I', and when the source is calling, in that moment of 'Absolute Divine Truth', it would happen; it needs no effort like any other universal truth." I wish to elaborate this wisdom because it is time to say no to lies, it's time to take charge of our being. It is time to attain moksha, maybe not from the cycle of life and death, but surely from lies and untruth. Let me break it down for you.

Truth 1: They say salvation can be attained as a result of practice! Don't you think if that is so, then everyone should do that for 50 years or maybe 50 lifetimes (that is if the soul is a real dud), get it right once and for all, and finally say goodbye to earth school? I am sure souls like Gurus and Lamas would be able to nail it in just a few lifetimes, but then even the Dalai Lama is the 14th reincarnation of a great Buddhist 'Avatar', hence proved it does not work like that. There can be no one way to salvation and neither to enlightenment.

Truth 2: There is no going up or above. Ascend or descend, there is only going within. Every spiritual (non-religious) scripture, all Sufi saints say: to know Him you must know yourself. So I wonder how and why you would be going up or anywhere to know yourself. The human mind, being linear, believes up is somewhere outside of it. Up or above means a higher, more open, expansive dimension of your self. Ups and downs are levels and dimensions of your consciousness, existing at all times, at all places, and within you. It is your intention, your willingness to see and access it that makes it available to you. As you heal and drop the clutter, you have gathered, and when your inner eye searches your truth, you get to access more of this vast consciousness. That is when you hold yourself higher in your soul's eyes, and that is what is called ascension. Everything is happening within you and at all times. The more you clear yourself, the more you get in touch with the source within; you would slowly see and feel the source's presence within and without. There is nowhere to go and nothing to attain, but to dissect and see yourself under a microscope, and finally connect with that divine essence.

Truth 3: The reason why you can never attain salvation by doing the practices that you believe lead to it is no rocket science. What is salvation? Freedom from all attachments and that which keeps you stuck here. When you practice anything with an expectation of results attached to it, aren't you getting attached to the outcome? Then there is attachment, isn't it? So first free yourself from this attachment. Can you? When there is attachment, there can be no freedom. Period.

Truth 4: Moksha is freedom from all the states of you, but the method is all-inclusive, and not at all excluding. You see, recognise, acknowledge, embrace, realign and reorient yourself with all the good, excellent, pure, bad, dirty, ugly and sinful you, which would free you from your identification with your judgements and conclusions of who and how you, others and the whole of this universe should be.

***

3

Twice Born

If you have only been born once, you will die twice. But if you have
been Born Twice you will only die once.

—Steven Lawson

In the spiritual process of ascension, realisation or whatever
we may call it, there is a phenomenon called 'Twice Born.' I had
never heard of it till I met one of my mentors when I was neck-
deep in trouble, during my second knock-off in May 2016.

I still remember very vividly. It was December 19, 2015; I
was sitting at the dining table enjoying a yummy Persian meal
with my brother and his wife. We were pulling each other's leg
over childhood memories when for a moment, just for a fraction
of a second, I had a vision of a 'light' that felt like a male presence
and looked rather cute. He measured approximately one-
foot in height with a compact structure in silvery-white light.
He appeared right in front of me, hovering over my favourite
saffron-berry rice dish.

I was putting a spoon of the aromatic rice, loaded with as
many berries as the spoon could accommodate in my mouth
when he appeared. 'He looks funny,' I thought to myself. But I

could sense a firmness in the energy; I immediately recognised it was something serious. It was a sense of knowing, back then I wasn't yet clairaudient; I used to receive the energy and of course, I could see. He then said: "Your work is over, but you still have breaths, do you want to go or stay?"

I was taken aback and too shocked to react. In that split second (if there is a way to measure such a small unit of time) I had two thoughts running in my mind simultaneously. The first thought was—my brother and his wife are guests here, they know nothing about how to get a burial done, and I want to be buried in Iran, on my land, but it would be so much of a hassle for them to take the body back to Iran.

The second thought was a memory that showed up. I remembered one of my mentors tazelling us in a seminar: "It is always better to stay longer and complete as much work as possible than having too many short reincarnations." As these thoughts were running in my mind, I wasted no time in replying. Knowing that my current life was not planned by myself, I wanted to be sure I would not go wrong again. I replied, "I will stay to do more work, but only if you take care of all future karma. You will not allow me to generate any negative karma. I don't know how, but you need to make sure I do not create any negative karma; you stop me from meeting people, doing things or going places. I don't know how; you figure that out. If you do that, only then would I stay and do more work."

I felt a naughty smile, and this time I heard a voice. "DONE," he said and disappeared. While this was going on, which at that time felt like an eternity, everything around me had dissolved. I could see a haze as if a thick fog had engulfed everything around me. Time seemed to have frozen. As soon as the 'Light Being' disappeared, everything looked so bright, colours felt so much brighter, and everything looked sharp. It took me more time to gather myself from what I had just experienced than it took me to make a deal with a 'Spirit Guide.' I could no more eat, so I put the spoon down. I didn't know what this experience meant at that point; I was utterly baffled. I just knew I had never had such an experience before, and probably, would never have in the future.

I had had many beautiful spiritual experiences, each of them unique and filled with wisdom as well as everlasting energy shifts. They were deep 'AHA' moments, which opened beautiful new doors of wisdom, but this experience was intense in a very unusual way. When I gathered myself, I looked at my brother and his wife's faces to check if they had noticed anything odd about me. They looked normal, continuing with the same conversation. I looked at their plates trying to figure out the elapsed time, but to my surprise, it seemed that on the physical plane I had not missed even a second.

There are no words to match how that experience felt; it has left a lasting impression on me, one that cannot be described. As I type these words, the feeling, and the memory of the exchange of information that took place in the subjective spiritual dimension while my body was fully present and active in the objective physical realm, is alive with the same intensity. I kept on mentally revisiting what had happened for a week and then decided not to remain stuck with the experience and made an effort to forget it. I knew, what I was supposed to know or do would unfold in due time, no point remaining there. The occurrence felt too strange to even mention to anyone. I had not understood what exactly it meant, and slowly I forgot about it until four months later.

It was late in March 2016, during a 'Family Constellation'

workshop, when I was reminded of the cute guide. We had finished the workshop well in time; in fact, we had an hour extra. I decided to do a therapy for myself, and my clients and students welcomed the idea. Usually, people have a sense of curiosity to know about the therapist and how they do their stuff; what is the level of their progress etc. I could sense the excitement in the air. I had a straightforward question: I wanted to know and heal the cause of the extreme body heat I had been feeling, which was very unusual for me. Despite some healing and mild therapies, the condition would reoccur after a few days or maximum a week.

During the winter, it was a great feeling, but with the arrival of spring, I had started to feel uneasy. No amount of healing was helping. I felt as if my muscles were melting inside; my skin had become very thin and irritable. It was so bad that people sitting next to me could feel the heat. Once before, I had a similar feeling, which was a Kundalini experience, and it was healed, but this one was extremely uncomfortable. I felt as if my skin was being ripped apart. The body being our most honest and faithful friend, I decided to know what it was trying to tell me. The first thing as a therapist one asks is—what's wrong? Where have I deviated from the path that my body is in so much discomfort?

For the uninitiated, here is some information. 'Family Constellation' and 'Soul Macrocosm Drama' are therapies where the issue is unfolded and healed through role-plays. The theory behind this super-powerful and accurate therapy is that our life is a result of our perception. Often challenges are due to our lack of understanding of the situation as it was originally designed; once on earth, we do not remember the route map, and we tend to look at life as per our already-in-place programming or conditioning. During this therapy, the person gets to witness the reason behind the challenge, which shifts the perception and brings about the resolution.

That day too, like all other times, I chose a person who would represent me as a process. Once in the therapy grid, she mentioned she needed to lie down. I offered her the couch, and she immediately took a foetal position with her knees close to her chest and head bent towards the knees. Initially, I did not understand; even though it looked like a foetus, I was a bit apprehensive, so I asked her why she was lying down in that position. She replied, "I am in the womb!" She then went on to say: "Don't you remember the old man? The one who asked you on the dining table if you wanted to go or stay? You said you would stay; there is so much to do, so much work, you had to stay and do the work." Then she started crying; she seemed to be in a state of trauma. I asked her what makes her cry. She replied: "Because they manipulated me again. They made me stay. Is that a time to ask such a question without giving me time to think? And then they only put the memory of my teacher in my mind? They always do this with me. I am so exhausted. I wanted to sleep; my work was over." Once she calmed down, she continued; "I have no choice now, I was tricked into staying back so now I am in the womb again."

It took me a few seconds to recall the memory. I couldn't believe what I was hearing. Not a soul knew about that experience; in fact, even I had completely forgotten about it. I realised it was for real and more was to come, so I asked her what did that conversation mean? She then explained the whole episode. The 'light being' was for real; I had made a deal with the 'Realm of Spirit.' I had bartered my breaths for doing more service—future karma. The lady representing me repeated the entire mental conversation between the 'Guide' and me on that day of December 2015. She then explained; my skin was irritable as the babies in the womb initially have no skin and, of course, you feel everything in magnitude. The heat was because the womb is a warm place. She then asked me, "Don't you see—you can no more digest food?"

She was right; it had been almost three months since I could no more digest food; the only food I was eating for breakfast, lunch and dinner was boiled bottle gourd. It was so odd that even my help at home had asked me a few times why I was not tired of the same food? I had attributed this to conscious eating, and thinking I was eating what my body desired. That constellation was the beginning of many more works, which showed the way forward step by step. It clearly mentioned what and when was the next thing to be done. I had a guide map of how to take care of myself during this period, but no information was revealed about the work or the new 'Soul Plan.' The next few months were harsh; I was experiencing extreme physical discomfort, change in sleep patterns, lack of energy and much more.

Each time new information would be disclosed, guidelines were given to the T. Initially, I was a bit apprehensive, but the next session happened in Mumbai, with a new set of people who didn't know me. Yet, the person representing me would pick up the story from where I had left it in the previous session. These messages and the way they were carried out made me believe in what was happening. Mentally it wasn't easy; it was a period of eternal wait and adventure. The curiosity of knowing what's next made me do over 20 therapy workshops in just about two months. It was adding to my physical discomfort, as each time a deep therapy like that takes place, there are always multi-layers of energy shifts that take place for all participants. The physical body being denser and having its limitation, takes more time to adapt to the new levels of energy.

Everything was exciting and happening as per plan till May 19, 2016, when the Foreigner Registration Office in Chandigarh gave me a second call, stating my exit order had been issued for the second time. During the period from May 19 to December 29 of that year, the day I was granted my Indian citizenship, I experienced a living nightmare. That period till the end of 2017 was the darkest night of my soul. In between all the rounds of attending court hearings, visiting the foreign registration office in my city and the Ministry of Home Affairs at New Delhi, in between all the countless emails, letters and long waits outside different offices, I was working day and night to heal the situation. It was a period of extreme testing, even though there is no God to test us!

Amid all the crying and praying, helplessness and hopefulness, I received a very profound message that helped me change my perspective and hence heal the situation. Since I was always out of the house, I used to be at Sukhna Lake quite often. There is a beautiful tree there, a few hundred years old, with which I made a deep connection. One day, I was meditating under the tree and felt it had a message for me. I opened my eyes and touched its root, and the tree whispered: "The size of your troubles is proportionate to the size of your ego. Let go of your stubborn anger with life, and you shall be set free of the test of your ego; life does not test anyone, what are you trying to prove and to whom?" I always knew I had chosen the pain and knew I was the solution, but I had this programming that God puts us to the test. My beautiful friend—the tree—erased that programming for me, forever. It opened the knot.

Have you ever been through a situation where you felt you had nothing to lose? When you felt so soul-shaken and beaten that nothing else ever mattered? I was exactly there. I was angry with God, with the universe, with myself, with authorities and yet so deeply grateful for the beautiful support system, amazing friends and profound learning. I was continuously drowning in anger and frustration, but at the same time flying in gratitude and glory. I knew something massive was taking place behind the scenes, and the stage was being prepared. Yet, I could not fathom the fact that whoever was God, had no mercy on my human limitations and sometimes even no understanding of what all a human is capable of. Today I know, it was all wrong. Human beings are infinite potencies and 'So Am I.'

We all might have reached testing times when it is hard to decide if one is more beaten, broken or shattered. I was there. I knew I was shattered and beaten, but refused to accept I was broken. That for sure was not a choice. Therefore, I chose to stand, pause, breathe and get back right on my feet marching back into the battlefield, determined to please God and pass with flying colours.

I lived almost like a criminal for 40 days, without having done anything wrong. I would leave my house at 6 am and come back at 11 pm; for some strange reason, I had a fear of being arrested even though technically and logically I had nothing to worry about. All my papers were in place, all my facts were clear, but perhaps the universe has its crazy ways of pushing people over the edge; it helps teach them how to take a leap of faith. I was there, right at the edge and had no choice but to jump.

One day I remember sitting with a friend asking him, why would I have chosen this? I haven't ever done anything illegal or harmed anyone. At this stage, when my citizenship has been approved, why would the government issue an exit order for me? It was two months later that I got to know that no such order was ever issued. It was the FRRO officer who was hand-in-glove with my ex, and this was an attempt to bring me to panic mode so that I would be forced to leave on my own. Yet, as the universe had designed everything for me to heal, I had decided to fight it tooth-and-nail instead of leaving in fear. I was feeling frustrated and helpless, as no one was ready to hear me out. India is a great land, but like any other place, sometimes there are wrong people in positions of power that truly can be a disaster for someone who wants to obey the rules, and that is what exactly was going on in my life.

I was squeezed from everywhere. Attending two, sometimes three court hearings every week, shuttling between New Delhi and Chandigarh, endless waiting hours that sometimes would last over two-three days, to beg the officer-in-charge to have a look at my file. Once my friend and I ran out of both money and clean clothes, as we waited from 8 am to 6 pm to meet the concerned officers for six days in a row. We eventually drove back to Chandigarh. As we touched the border of Chandigarh, I got a call that we had been given an appointment for the next day at 8 am. It was a chaotic time, but thanks to a beautiful support system I managed to sail through. The last blow below my belt was when the FRRO revoked my work permit in July that year. Above all, my physical condition got worse due to the spiritual process. As I was writing this book, it was two years past that time and I was still recovering,

That period was by far the most turbulent I ever faced; it was perhaps the healing time for my spirit to start recognising its true power slowly. I must confess it took me a while to balance myself. My biggest learning from that time was to remain 'centred' at all times and always have faith that there is a bigger plan at work, so never to feel helpless. The vulnerability of helplessness can take you deep into the dungeons of unawareness. I was doing everything within my capacity, and maybe beyond, to bring the situation under control.

"It is a tough time, but I am tougher," I kept telling myself. I did every possible thing, both at the physical as well as the spiritual level, to heal what I had chosen. It was during one such healing that another beautiful truth was revealed. A 'Guide' appeared and explained to us that not all Soul Plans are decided by the souls. He mentioned that sometimes the 'Soul plan' is decided by the Guides. I was then shown how I did not wish to revisit the earth, believing I had already completed my lessons, whereas the 'Council of Elders' believed that I still had unfinished business and had to go back. I could feel my fury and sticky resistance in LBL stage, and yet aware that I had no choice. I only chose the outcome and not the exact plan. I was then explained the extent of free will at the realm of 'Spirit', and things started to get clearer for me. During this period, I had tried connecting to a couple of my mentors for help, but no one responded. It was in July 2016 during a spiritual conference at New Delhi when I spoke to one of my teachers, a very brief conversation. I explained my situation; he looked into my eyes and said, "You are a light worker, hold on tight. You are being 'Twice Born'".

I didn't understand much, I needed more of a solution than a spiritual, confusion-loaded statement, but at that moment, something inside me ignited. I thought to myself it was my battle, I would fight it till I could, and for the joy of winning it, if that's in my destiny. I did over 21 constellations, countless energy healings, saw about seven-eight past lives, all in search of the key to this one issue, which was practically all of my life. With each session, a knot would get untied, a beautiful knowing would show up, but the issue would remain unresolved. In the meanwhile, in the physical reality, many shifts were taking place. I had changed three lawyers; once my case had got dismissed because the lawyer who had taken money never appeared in the court, so there was no one to explain the case. At one point, it felt it was all over. Finally, I was advised to consult Mr Ashwini Chopra, who restored my faith, not only in the judiciary and the law but also in humanity and goodness.

I do believe in 'earth angels' and Mr Chopra for sure is one of them. The gift of all these challenges was that I was made to meet a few angelic people, whom my soul would cherish for all eternity.

Post-July 2016, I started to notice small changes taking place. As I was healing and shifting within, so was my world. I was having new openings, supportive and beautiful people showing up randomly all the time (even in those places where I had only experienced injustice before). I had a beautiful support system after 21 years, which I consider the most valuable gift of life; all these changes where an indication that a shift was taking place, yet my lessons were incomplete. I knew unless I learn the lessons, the challenge won't resolve. I knew it was only me who could do it. I decided to face it all; hence, I told my friends I would attend all the court hearings alone and would meet the officials alone too—I had to face my fears. There was no short cut; I had done the escaping game long enough. Whatever it was, it was between me and authorities; we all know who the ultimate authority is— God, Source, AHA! (I used the term God often then.)

I had to heal with God or someone who represented him. I was angry with God for the manipulation; as I write this, I find it hilarious, but that was me then, and I want you to know how stupid we all can be.

During the next constellation, I was asked to do a ritual at a particular date and time, during which I was given a name too. The beauty is how everything was arranged for me to do the ritual. The process was to be done at a particular time and finish at a set time. I had no idea how I was supposed to do the work. The next day a friend dropped by from New Delhi; she had been abreast of the whole work that was going on. She said she was missing our talks, so she had just driven down to meet me and would go back the same day. I casually asked her about the ritual, and she said that her mother was trained in 'Hindu Rituals.' She found out the Sanskrit chants; her mother sang them melodiously and sent the audio files to us.

As we were talking, another dear friend messaged me about some challenges she was facing with her sister. When I called her, she mentioned some critical point related to the ritual as a part of her challenge summary. In the next six hours, I not only knew how to do it but also all the other arrangements were made. The next day I woke up at 4:30 am and completed the ritual. Once I was done, and before I could check the time, the alarm I had scheduled to let me know about the exact time went off. And I was 'Twice Born'—in the same body.

Our physical age in our lifetime, and how long we stay in this school called Earth, is determined by the number of our breaths, not by the number of years. That is the reason why all Sadhus, Gurus and Yogis aim at mastering the breath. The longer and calmer each breath is, the longer and healthier our life would be.

Death happens only if either our breaths or our work is over. By work, I mean completion of the pre-decided karma and learning lessons the soul had chosen.

If you run out of breaths while you haven't learnt your lessons, you will come back with the same karma and the same lessons; just that it would get tougher. Usually, a soul repeats an unlearnt lesson and completes it in a karmic cycle. A karmic cycle consists of 108 lifetimes. However, I have seen souls who did not learn the same lesson over nine or ten karmic cycles. The other possibility of exiting this world before time would be cases of suicide or when some people start interfering with the 'Divine Plan.' In such cases, the universe assassinates you, and you are removed from this existence swiftly and smoothly, without a second thought.

As much as it feels strange, now I understand being 'Twice Born' is not really a great deal. It's just the completion of the karmic cycle and moving to the next lesson in the same body. What happened to me is that 'I managed to finish my work much before I ran out of breath.' That would have happened to many others who we may not know of. I still don't know if that is a good thing or a bad thing. I do know it is a lot of work.

Finally, I have understood we are here to have joy; we are on this earth to work right, not hard. We're here to party real hard, but do it in line with our awareness and with the highest good of all, respecting and honouring boundaries as we have this vast playground of life. We must adhere to the rules of life while we live fully. So keeping that in mind, I wonder if being twice-born is a good thing. As a life coach, I train my clients to work smart, not hard. It is working smart that is fun and makes them more productive. It seems my soul, too, has been aware of this fact.

I was always a hard worker because that had been my

conditioning. My parents programmed me with a few disastrous programs, and one of them was: 'You need to work hard to achieve anything.'

It is only recently that I have learnt to work smartly and pay attention to the fun aspect more than anything else in my work; however, I feel the divine and my soul together chose to work smart. Constellations would have been my smart bites despite my hard-work programming. Constellations expanded my knowing in leaps and unimaginable bounds.

If someone had told me that one could be born twice in the same body even five years ago, I would have referred him to a seasoned psychiatrist. But today I have learnt never to judge anyone, never ridicule a possibility. Not only because of my story but after all the cases I have witnessed, I have learnt and now tell everyone to be open to every possibility. This beautiful universe is kind, generous and innovative. It can offer you the same thing in a billion ways, so ask and be open to receive; never think of how.

It was a few weeks after my re-birth in October 2016; while I was in meditation, I had the blessings of a 'Master.' He told me to forget about my challenges; he just said, "You do your work by taking care of my people, and I will take care of you." I knew I had to trust him, but I didn't know how. The only way was to try and replace my fear with faith consciously.

That week I had to attend a court hearing and travel to New Delhi to meet the foreigner's director. When I met him, he told me he had five minutes to hear me out. After hearing me for five minutes, he decided to know my story in detail. He called for my file and asked his personal assistant to take the minutes of the meeting (he was another beautiful soul I met). After eight years of running from pillar to post and trying to make someone to at least hear my ordeal, this was a miracle. I couldn't believe what I was hearing. He not only listened to me but also assured me of going through my file, and if he felt, after verifying the facts, that my case was genuine, he would reinstate my permission to work. He said, "You would know my decision in 48 hours, whether positive or negative." For me, this was a victory; finally, I could present my case, and I was heard.

At that moment, what mattered was that I had broken a barrier, someone had heard me. I knew the 'Master' was keeping his promise and that I was on the right track.

When I appeared in the next court date, there was a document which was received. My work permit was re-issued. It was a great relief; I could resume working. The next time the same 'Master' showed his presence, he asked me to surrender completely. In very clear instructions, I was conveyed that I would not be going anywhere anymore. The messages were short, firm and direct.

Of course, I did not argue. But even imagining I would inform Mr Chopra that I would no more be attending the court hearings was impossible. It took me a few visualisations, loads of mental effort and some rehearsal to finally speak to Mr Chopra. It was a lot more difficult to tell my friend Smriti (another Angelic soul to whom I am deeply grateful) who had put in as much effort, if not more, to help me and be by my side, that 'despite all your efforts to help me with appointments, I am sorry, I won't be going anywhere to meet anyone.'

It felt insane, rude and disrespectful to their efforts. After a few days of thinking, apprehending and rehearsals, I contacted my lawyer to tell him that I won't be attending any more court hearings. To my surprise, he agreed and said, "You have already done enough, I understand." I then called Smriti and informed her about my entire experience. She assured me I was not needed, and since she was in New Delhi, she would be representing me. There were a few court dates, which I missed purposefully. My next court hearing was on December 29, 2016, which of course, I was going to miss; it was the day of the decision.

I remember I had not slept the whole night. Since I could not take the anxiety anymore, I decided to go for a walk to Sukhna Lake at 4:30 am. I got back from the walk and was sitting by the window. My heart was beating in my mouth, and my chest felt empty. I could feel my whole nervous system exploding. I was doing my best to slow down the breath and manage my nerve-wracking stress, which was now on the rooftop (years later, my muscles are still recovering from the near breakdown situation I went through during those seven months) when my phone rang.

It was my landlord calling. I wondered why she was calling so early. As soon as I said hello, Mrs Sharma said, "Congratulations, Sahar, you are now an Indian Citizen." I couldn't believe, as there were still four hours left for the court to open, and usually, after the decision is made, it takes a couple of weeks for the pronouncement of the decision. I didn't know what to say; my mind was racing with a few questions when she said, "I am sending you the newspaper. There is a headline—'An Iranian woman has been issued Indian citizenship'".

Even though I had felt numb for many years, I could feel something—an unusual mix of joy and disbelief. I felt the freshness of the morning winter air in my lungs as if breathing for the first time. Twelve years of pain rolled down my eyes in the form of tears; tears of joy, tears of freedom. Our heart is such a beautiful organ; the song in it may not be heard, but it never dies. I could hear the song of my heart that day. There was a lightness in everything, and the first question was now what? I had been so busy surviving and fighting that suddenly my mind was feeling knocked out with emptiness.

When I look back, 'Surrender' has been by far the hardest lesson of all. This period and the next year till end-2017 was a period of extremes. The last cutting process of the diamond I was meant to be. The polishing is still on and, perhaps, is a never-ending job, but I am certain the heating and the cutting is over. Each one of us is hiding a beautiful jewel within us; we are just unaware. It takes some work, patience, kindness; sometimes heat and cutting for it to be recognised. The beauty is, you are the only one who has to find and cherish it. You are the only one who can value it first and put it to use, but no one taught us that.

All we have been taught has been about how to be good to others, how to be nice to others; how to be kind, obedient, good and patient with others. And how to love others. No one has taught us how to behave with ourselves. No one told us to love, be kind and gentle with ourselves too. Strange, isn't it?

The period of turmoil I went through was a close encounter with the process of 'Surrender.' I was brought to the point that my ego had no other choice. My best bet would have been surrender. Two years down the line, I am still learning. I am continuously checking and practising surrender. To my understanding, surrender is synonymous with absolute faith, where you face your fear in its eye and say, "I see you, but guess what? You are passé! I have someone much bigger than you having my back and pushing me forward." The best thing about surrender is that it works.

Fear disappears. Unlike what most people think, surrender has nothing to do with becoming passive and refraining from taking action. It means to let go of fear. It is about letting go of the need to control. It can happen only as a package deal; it is a process that cuts through your fears with the sword of faith. It is moment-by-moment living; it is being in the present; as Eckhart Tolle says, 'When in surrender, you have great dreams and determined plans. When in surrender you are assertive with the input, totally detached from your once envisioned output.' It's like a manufacturing unit with a macro design, equipped with the best resources working on auto mode. Whatever goes into this production unit has no choice but to come out as the best combination that could ever be, even if it looks alien. You must know that always 'The Best' would come out; however, there are a few conditions.

First, the input that is your intention and efforts have to be best, and for the highest good of all. Second, you must be aware of the process that's your awareness of you at every moment. Third, have no expectations of an outcome, keep the vision alive and be open to receiving in any manner, from anyone or anywhere. You may desire it, visualise it, but don't get obsessed with it. Surrender is about being in absolute allowance of what's coming, despite what you may desire from a space of inner knowing that: 'All is always well, I am safe and no matter what it is, it is always happening for me, not against me.'

I hear people talk about absolute surrender. I tell you it is nonsense. There is nothing absolute in this universe. Because nothing ever is, everything is constantly becoming, nothing is ever complete, yet everything is always perfect. That is the nature of the universe and this existence. It is not only you and me; the entire existence is a work in progress. The desire to have complete surrender in itself is the cause of your suffering. Whatever degree of surrender it is, it is just perfect for this moment. Because everything is just perfect the way it is, at the moment of your perception of it. It shall only get better moment-by-moment, always perfect, yet never complete, as there is always infinite scope for improvement. Whether you like it or not, everything is always changing for the better and getting better, unless you bring yourself in between and block its growth and improvisation by your rigid perception.

Let me tell you a secret—if you can surrender to your breath and live every moment fully present in that moment and with yourself, you would have been in complete surrender at that moment.

In the present moment, there CANNOT be any fear; only faith resides in the present, no pain of the past, no worry of the future. Worry is the domain of the future. The very present moment is filled with the progeny of faith, joy and grace. Your job is to surrender to that moment and then pick the next moment, and then the next, as they present themselves to you.

Today, I do believe I am 'Twice Born.' The new me is a very different person and still a work in progress, but a conscious one. From my nationality to the way I see life and deal with it, everything has changed. I am a 'New Me.' There has been a birth of a new level of consciousness, a new knowing; a new sense of freedom that is incomparable with anything else I have ever known. This new self is more aware of the 'Soul Self', is more fun-loving and easy-going, as if all my programming has been reset. I so love this new me. The game has changed from 'I to We' and from 'Me to Us.' It is a great feeling even though I keep a close check to make sure I don't trip. I know the 'Ego Self' is always waiting for a crack to peep in and slowly enter. I am watchful.

This new dimension is a place of knowing, where finally

I recognise that I know nothing, or even better, the new me doesn't even know if I don't know anything at all. The new me is so certain about uncertainty being the truth and is so complete in not knowing, and yet being ever so curious. It is a space where 'neither knowing nor not knowing' does not matter anymore. What I know for sure is that irrespective of what I know or do not know, I am perfect. Nothing can ever contain or define me, as I am constantly growing, and I am certain all is always well and happening for me at all times.

The pain and pleasure of knowing that all that has happened in my life, no matter how it felt then, was always in my support, is ecstatic. This new 'me' is a dimension of knowing—that I am the beginning, the end, and all that happens in-between. The desire to end suffering has to be sown by me alone, watered by me alone, and it will bloom for me alone. For a very long time and till very recently, I blamed a God outside of me, who watched me suffer and did nothing despite all his might. He watched this poor good girl, who went through all suffering—without making a noise—and yet did not do anything. I had so much anger towards this useless 'Supreme Power' outside of me that it took me a dozen anger release sessions and a few past lives to release the rage I was carrying. The new 'me' laughs at my ignorance each time it catches me giving my power away, or ignoring my awareness.

One day Smriti and I were talking our 'usually unusual' talks when I realised the out of proportion anger I displayed in certain situations was a 'soul level' rage. I recognised my soul was furious, and the next thing to work on was my soul's fury. I realised that this, if not dealt with as an SOS situation, could burn a whole forest. It took me a month of rigorous self-work, introspection, checking and re-checking the anger in all aspects to get back.

Today, I know that I am His essence, the very 'Source' that resides in everything and everyone is residing in me too. The beauty of this Source/God/Energy is that once it enters any container, it becomes that. I learnt that the Source in me had become me. It was behaving as per my beliefs—allowing me to be in the full experience of the trash I had gathered in my past, so much in allowance of what I have ever been, yet nudging me towards him once again. It wasn't the 'Source' but me who didn't believe I deserved love. It was me who felt unworthy of joy; it was me who believed in hard work, and who had blocked grace. It was me who believed in self-punishment. I was filled with guilt and shame, ashamed of who I was and my past—so-called sins—from across lifetimes.

My Creator had no judgement about me. It was waiting for me, allowing me to find out for myself that I have been wrong all this while; that there were no sins and that I was as special as anyone else, never separated from it. I realised the Source loves each one of us so much that it could never say no to us. It not only allows us what we desire but mimics what we believe to the T so that we can have a full plate of what we need to experience and learn. And that acceptance and allowance are what we term as unconditional love.

We all are 'God' essence. We all are an expression of this abundant Source; made in his image with total love and devotion. Yet we have a choice to believe and represent it or deny and reject it. As crazy as it may sound, but we all are gods on earth. We are the Creator of our universe. All that we need to do is to choose to 'Act Like One.' It is not so difficult to realign to your Godness. All that you need to do is to seek to know in every situation—if the Source was to deal with the challenge, how easily it could be resolved. What energy should you be to invite graceful possibilities which would resolve the issue as if by magic? Only asking questions would open doors.

Let me give you a few clues to start with.

To slowly pave the way back to yourself and your God essence, you need to remember that the Source does not judge anything or anyone as good or bad, right or wrong. It is present in all, from microbes and viruses, living and non-living, angels and demons at the same level, and in all aspects. To the Source, the entire creation is fairly important, and at the same time, equally dispensable. Everything is unique and beautiful. It has no identity and can become whatever contains it. It does not force you to do anything you do not wish. It works around you and with you, but NOT on you. All its focus is on the evolution of consciousness and nothing else. The Source is always open to change; it is supportive of growth and helps those who help themselves. It never interferes and always answers if called. To express your Godness in all that you do, keep these points in mind. Remember, there is a thin line between representing the Creator that is recognising your truth, which is that you are powerful beyond measure, and trying to become the Creator. You for sure are the Creator, but only of your reality. Don't become the God of others. Why people lose their sense of knowing is because human consciousness, our mind, is always seeking to identify with everything. What we identify with is not real. Our reality is nothing but an illusion, based on what we already know, rooted in what we wish to believe and have confirmed, or stemming out of our search for what we miss. Does it sound confusing? Let me explain.

It is simple, you would not brag about what or who you are. A king would not go around and tell everyone how it feels to be a king; he does not have to brag about it because he is it, and everyone either knows it or would know. He does not have to do anything about it to prove to anyone. We all have stories with which we identify the most; they are mostly either sob stories or stories of glories.

It does not matter what your story is; you repeat it because you are not it. You either believe it to be true or wish people to believe it as your truth. Both display the need for attention and love. We exhibit power when we feel a threat. We desire to possess what we are certain we don't have or don't have enough of. Being realised is the same thing; you neither wish others to know about it, nor is there a need to exhibit it. Realisation is about dropping the self. It is the self that identifies with all the stories. The soul already is all of it.

Once realised, all desires drop; what remains is an innate and equally intense yearning to discover more of who you are. The desire to live a full life does not come from a place of need or greed. It is not because you want to have, possess or achieve, but because you wish to expand your being. You wish to cocreate with the Creator for the fun and joy of it. All that you wish is to experience its presence in all that you do and allow him to explore, and express, using you as a vessel.

At this stage in evolution, the self has disappeared into nothingness, and this nothingness that you have become holds the entire existence effortlessly. It no more matters if all is lost or all is gained, what matters is inhaling life in full capacity and exhaling life into full-size creation. Every inhalation is a session of love-making with life; every exhalation an orgasmic adventure.

Every single belief, all your stories and dogmas would disappear in-between the silky sheets of your truth, where your body, mind and soul are constantly coming in touch with the softness of life, making love to every moment, impregnating every desire with love for all.

The erotic dance of this existence is not only visible to you, but it invites you to bed the entire creation, exploring more of your beauty that is mingling with life with each breath. You are in ecstasy. As much as it is seductive and desirable, it is also a frightening realisation. It takes a lot of effort to keep remembering and reminding yourself that you are the Creator of your reality. It is scary to admit what all you have done to yourself and even more terrifying to know every thought, word and action of yours is constantly either creating or destroying you.

In the initial stages of this knowing, there would be times you would wish and pray if it could be reversed. You would want to still believe in a God outside of you. You may even regret reaching where you have reached, wondering if it was worth it at all. It would take a while and then slowly you would submit yourself to the fact that: 'It has always been you and will always be about you; only you.' That no one ever punished you or planned anything against you—but you-yourself. You would finally surrender to the fact that you have no choice but to take responsibility and be accountable for your past, present and the eternity of your being. That is a phase of struggle with self. It is unbelievably difficult to accept that all the self-induced pain could have been avoided if you would have just remained aware. Once your struggle phase of acceptance is over, you would feel a new freedom. You recognise yourself as a free 'Spirit', open to potent possibilities and benevolent choices. And you are BORN AGAIN!

4

Know the Truth of Death

To be born again is what we all are doing, all the time. Our body is continuously regenerating itself. Millions of cells are dying and being replaced in our body every day. Nature keeps moving from birth to death and birth again, with each new season. Nothing in this universe fears death as much as humans do. Our mind fears death, not realising death merely is a platform for growth. I remember when I was six-and-a-half years old, my paternal grandfather died. I watched my father when he was mourning. I was bewildered, seeing everyone crying. I had just heard my mother and my aunt explaining to my elder brother, and another cousin, that Grandpa had gone to visit God and now he would be living there. My little mind was quite baffled as to why going to God was a bad thing? Or why were they so sad? God would look after him better, I thought to myself. When I asked my mother about it, she said because they would miss him, which back then I did not quite understand.

The age of 14 was very significant for me; I had my first experience of awakening. Something was happening, and the first sign was I started having precise predictions. One day while checking my younger brother's homework, I looked at him and told him that I felt our grandmother would cross over the next Thursday. My brother, being attached to her, looked at me in disbelief and said, "How cold are you? How can you say something like that so calmly when you know most things you say happen?" I had no answer to that then. But one thing I knew was I could not relate to death the way others did.

When my grandmother died, for two-three days, I had to pretend sadness and force myself to mourn, that made me feel sick about myself, so I decided to take over the kitchen to avoid acting. But I had already started judging myself and started thinking maybe I really am cold-blooded or maybe there is some defect in me. I stayed with this and later each time I would hear about the death of someone, I would go back and check my feelings, till one day I realised I was actually happy for them. Finally, they had left for a better place.

The age of 19, by the time I lost my paternal uncle and aunt, to whom I was closest, I was pretty sure that something was wrong with me. I always felt I loved them, if not more but equal to my parents, and yet I could not mourn. I did miss them, but there was no sadness. By the time I was in my late 20s after watching how people had reacted to death and their association with death, I had started to feel abnormal. It had become a question I desperately needed an answer to. I was always in distress, asking myself: 'Was I a bad person, a cold fish? Someone who was not loving or compassionate enough?'

I even attended a workshop on 'death and dying' to understand what was wrong with me. Even though the content of the workshop was very reassuring, but when I asked the teacher about how I felt, she concluded that I had been through a death trauma in childhood when I could not grieve properly, so I must have been frozen. That wasn't the case. I did have a trauma-filled childhood, but it had nothing to do with death.

I think my dysfunctional childhood had made me more fearful of life than death. After a few years more of staying with this question, I finally understood why I could not relate to death like others. I had had many lifetimes as monks, Sufis, etc.; I had also been a 'Shaman' who helped people suffering from painful diseases to cross over with ease. I realised those lifetimes, and the knowing I carried from those lifetimes, was the reason I could never relate to death as a loss or as a cause of separation. I was aligned with death as a process of life. That is how we fall prey to conformity, and we start doubting and judging ourselves when we don't fit the framework of society, and what others do or expect from us. I never felt my loved ones were gone; I would miss them because they were not available physically.

Interestingly, all of my deep friendships are the same. I don't miss people, but I have this assurance we are always connected. The connection I feel is beyond the physical presence.

Death is the beginning of an end and the end of a beginning. Nothing happens differently on the other side. You pick up the story exactly as how you left it. People think once you die, on the other side you change and become better. Well, that's not true.

As a therapist during every past life regression session, I invariably ask the subject to remember their last dying thought and to check what the lesson of that life was. Without fail, everyone recognises that the next life is the exact continuation of their last thought and how they felt. Someone who died of famine comes with lack-consciousness and a habit of hoarding for the rainy day. People who died with regret come back to learn how not to be regretful. Someone with shame comes back to learn to forgive the self. Death is a new chapter of your old book. Death is an art everyone must master. It is equally important to know how to die and also to let others die, as it is important to live and let others live.

We fear death so much that most of our life, we live to avoid death, ignoring the bliss of the journey. We dread this beautiful process, our only way forward, so much, that we forget to live. Our attachments cause us to find death painful, whereas we should celebrate the fact that our dear ones are moving forward in their growth.

It is important to let people who have crossed over to move forward in peace; it is important to let them go. I get many requests for channelling those who have crossed over from their loved ones, but that is interference with the laws of the universe. Those who have left this physical reality need to move to the dimension they belong to, and we must not delay them, we must not disturb them by calling them back again and again.

Death is a celebration we must indulge in.

***

5

Stay on the Path

Most of us, including me, have always been looking for answers in books or from teachers and mentors. That is a great start to our journey towards realisation. However, as I slowly moved into numerous turns of this journey, I realised nature, our body and our soul hold the answers to everything. The source has made so many simple clues for us to learn, to understand and to undo the knots, but we don't pay attention. It is important to know that everything that is in the physical realm is there because it had already existed in the dimension of the spirit—in the energy form. Nothing could become dense and appear to us unless it had already existed maybe for millions of years before we discovered it. Everyone can be 'Twice Born.'

Everyone can experience different dimensions of soul consciousness. It may be a rare phenomenon, but it surely can be duplicated. The processes and patterns of this universe are simple and easy; it is our mind that complicates the issue. Everyone, absolutely everyone, can shift and ascend his levels of consciousness while being in the same body; it is not exclusive to a select few. Some ingredients are an absolute must—to take responsibility, be willing and determined; to be open to guidance, to be diligent with the work you have undertaken and practice what you preach.

You need to take responsibility and own up your life. Your growth, your power and your potential are for you to claim. You need to own your shadows, as well as your light. The secret to growth at all levels is to know yourself and to own it up.

You also need to be willing to see, be, perceive and embrace your truth, willing to see deeper layers of yourself. Going to the depth of your being to those places you may have been dreading the most, willing to embrace the unknown.

Be open to guidance. Some guidance and hand-holding will take you a long way; however, being dependent on any teaching or any 'Guru' is nothing but your sign of resistance. You MUST be open to accepting the new, and be ready to drop the old, which no more serves you. Unlearning, dropping the old and decluttering yourself is the most difficult part of self-work, but it is an absolute must. That is where most people get stuck. It is because the mind operates from lack-consciousness; it hoards information. What if one day the information is required to save you? It just can't let go of anything. The truth is as you grow within, you realise 98 per cent of the information stored has become obsolete. The only way to move to the next level of your consciousness is by becoming lighter, dropping the weights of your all-knowing mind. You recognise that either the information or how you have been perceiving or processing it, all needs a major overhaul.

You need to be diligent and authentic with your self-work. 'Conscious awareness' is an essential ingredient of your soul food—awareness of your intentions, words, actions, feelings, reactions, stories and your patterns; and more than anything else, your 'shadow selves' which create your drama.

The self-work can't be just a part of your life, but the only way of life. Reading books, attending workshops, talks and hopping retreats are all great, but none, not even sleeping at the feet of your Guru is of any use, unless you apply what you have gathered in your life and not only sometimes, but always. You should breathe, eat, walk, talk and sleep what you have learnt.

I will share a few tools that have immensely helped many of my students and me; I am sure they will help you remain centred on your journey. You are anyways dying and being born again; my effort is to make you conscious of it. There is a joy in discovering yourself, and I am trying to contribute in a small way.

This process has helped thousands of my students and me, but don't be deceived by how simple it sounds! Like the Japanese Ikigai, it's simple to know but a herculean task to live by.

***

6

The Pause Button

Your Tool to Self-Discovery

PAUSE! No matter what happens in life and how it happens, no matter how challenging the times are and how urgently you need to act in life-and-death situations; no matter if it feels like 9/11 and if you don't act you will lose all the 72 virgins in heaven... take my word, just PAUSE.

Do not react. Do not assume. Do not judge. PAAAAAUUUUUSE! Stop doing all that you are doing and take a break; this can be anything from seven seconds to seven months! It does not matter; wait till you figure it all out in your sane mind.

There is a simple formula to practice the pause without letting your mind run into a hundred different directions. Take seven slow breaths or count seven seconds. Mentally count one thousand one, one thousand two...one thousand seven. Take a couple of deep breaths. You have succeeded to slow down your brain, remember our brain is most effective when it slows down. Now you can go back to the matter and see it from a better perspective. Sometimes you need to let matters rest at hand.

Practice being patient. Patience is not waiting; patience is doing your best, to be in charge while you have full faith—that no matter what's going on, the result is always going to be in your favour even if it is not what you desired or anticipated. When you learn how to be patient, it becomes a period of sweet learning, opening and unfolding. It no more carries the energy of frustration. When you wait in patience and with a deep sense of surrender as well as gratitude, you invite and allow the higher intelligence to show you the way, and also lead you to the best, shortest and fastest route. So take a pause.

Permit yourself to let go of control. Learn to trust life. Just shut down your system from what's going on. It is difficult but possible. That not only helps you ease your nerves but also allows new possibilities and fresh ideas to float. You would feel recharged and ready to get right back into action. The key is to do it from faith and not fear. Give yourself breathing space, be kind and gentle with yourself. I remember when I was going through a challenging learning phase when I knew I could stretch myself no more, I told everyone I was taking a break. I cancelled all my appointments, called off all my events and took a break from everything. I did have financial constraints. I did think a thousand times that people would think I was not reliable and did not honour my commitments. There were many insecure, fear-based thoughts hammering me. My mind was trying to force me to give in to fear, but I knew I had to practice what I preached. And guess what! No one felt that way. They understood, and if they did not, well, just too bad.

There would be a million more who would understand my needs and honour them. Ninety per cent of the people waited for me to come back after 72 days of silence. That just felt beautiful.

Heavens won't fall; neither the sun would be upset with you and stop shining the next day, nor would something happen which wasn't supposed to. If anything is to happen, it will happen anyway, and you possibly can't do anything about it. So stop thinking you are the centre of everything. Let's say even if you are, you can always decide what the job of this centre is. Just don't give in to chaos and fear. Trust me, it works.

***

7

The Gift of Introspection

If humanity had to be gifted just one superpower—it would be 'introspection.' I wish to share it with you so that you remain in charge of your life too. The one thing I can assure you is: 'The biggest gift to your soul is your ability to introspect.'

If you can search your soul deep enough and find out the intent behind every word you say, every gesture you make, every action you carry out; if you can pause and know how you are feeling precisely in any given situation; if you could know from which space you are operating at any given point, you are sorted. If you can be in touch with your feelings and intentions as you go about everything you do, you are almost resolved. Introspection helps you to connect the dots back and forth. Then the universe is no more compelled to present you with challenges to remind you of what you need to heal.

During one of our charity events, as I watched the smiles on people's faces, I felt a deep sense of joy. It was time for introspection. I wanted to know the intention behind what I was doing. Was this joy coming from a space of pride and ego? Was it the joy of sharing and gratitude? Or was my ego playing me in any way? Was I expecting gratification? It took me 15-20 minutes to check where exactly was I operating from.

Remember, it is your intention that brings you the experiences. If your intent or your beliefs are distorted, your experiences would be distorted too. You may use any technique, from therapies to merely asking questions; it does not matter how you do it but introspect you MUST.

I feel very blessed to have worked with different people from different walks of life, experiencing the beautiful divine love that exists within every human being. Even for those who may act evil or refuse to shine their divinity, in the end, it is all about love and being loved. There was a time when I realised that very difficult cases were knocking at my door, and I wondered what was bringing such people to me. As much as it was fun and challenging, and often great learning, some cases were very dense. When I looked within, I realised it was happening to me because I was operating from two powerful belief systems.

One, I believed I needed to overcome challenges to tell God how good I was, and the second was my need to experience extremities. Once I acknowledged my mind's stupidity, things changed significantly.

During one 'Soul Macrocosm Drama', suddenly after a few cases, the energy became unbearably heavy and dense. Everyone in the room could sense it. It took me a while to help the person open up. She confessed she was there not to heal, but to see how I do the work. It was something I needed to address; what in me was causing her to have unauthentic intentions in my environment. My first guess was, of course, maybe I had the wrong intentions. I paused the constellation and did one for myself. Apparently, in a past life, I was the follower of a cult where they believed the only way to salvation was through service and no matter who came with what intention, one had to serve even if it costed a life! That was precisely how I had died; I was made to serve at the cost of my health. I had died with the belief that maybe I didn't serve enough people; that I died such a death and I had to come back, so I had decided I would go back and serve no matter what. I had lost a sense of self-honour and boundary. At the time of death, I believed that my not achieving salvation was a punishment because I had not done enough. So my soul got more determined to serve and of course like attracts like; hence, I brought upon myself more of self-punishment, inviting people who would not honour me and my services in my environment.

Isn't it interesting how we carry millions of beliefs from the past, our environment and culture?

Identify your patterns and beliefs. Understand where you picked them from? How did you own them? Initially, it is tiring, soul-stirring and uncomfortable, but then slowly you start enjoying it. Each moment becomes like an 'AHA' moment. Nothing is more beautiful and fulfilling than discovering your own self. With each layer uncovered, a new 'you' emerges; more powerful, more loving and free. With each revelation, you shed a part of you that was dull and dirty; maybe it wasn't even you yet; perhaps you were burying your spark under the dust of self-doubt and disbelief. Nothing is absolute. Even while you are decluttering your mind and soul, everything has layers; so don't be quick in concluding.

For example, sadness and depression are the upper layers of unexpressed anger. Grief has helplessness and shock beneath it. Addiction is the top layer of lack of self-love and self-worth; the need to punish the self and escape this reality. Narcissism has extreme anger, self-hate, inferiority complex and rejection of the past.

Remember, this jewel you are searching for is so precious that you have hidden it beneath a thousand layers.

8

Acknowledge Yourself

Acknowledge yourself for who you are. Acknowledge your 'Soul', your 'Mind', your beautiful 'Body'. Pat yourself on the back; you have come a long way. You have been doing amazingly well, no matter where you are. You have survived all the obstacles, all the pain and sorrow, all the heart-breaks and soul-tearing loneliness. You have travelled a million miles, and you are here, at this very moment. Look at you. Your courage and resilience are commendable. You have made it so far, and you must acknowledge that.

Acknowledge your strengths, your weaknesses, your highs and your lows. Many of us have a problem with any eruption on the skin; usually, a pimple on the face bothers us. Sometimes losing hair is something which we do not like. Imagine people who don't like to see their 'physical being' as what they consider not so beautiful while you have had the courage to have a look at your soul with flashlights on—pointing out every eruption, pain and despair. Don't you think this calls for a celebration, an applaud? Remember, this is not the end, so keep going further and beyond, unless you fully dust the gem you are hiding inside, you won't be able to see the beauty of 'you.' Keep at it, see and acknowledge the liar, the lazy, the jealous, the narcissist, the super-ambitious, shrewd business owner. Acknowledge the greed, the sins and the forbidden fantasies, but also acknowledge the layers beneath. The one who is aching to be heard and noticed, to be cared and loved, the one who so wishes a soft touch and a warm hug and to be accepted for all that s/he is despite all that s/he has done. Unless you accept yourself as a whole, you won't find someone who will accept you for who you truly are; therefore, acknowledge and accept yourself completely and wholeheartedly.

You have no idea what hidden treasures you have got. So don't get excited too soon. Appreciate what you have unravelled and know there is much more for you to uncover. Take your time and do one thing at a time, but don't stop. Don't look at what others are doing and how they are doing. Learn from everyone and yet follow your awareness. Don't be scared; you are the light in the tunnel, it's just that you haven't seen it yet.

Every difficult person or situation you are encountering is merely a trigger because you called for it. If you remain aware, they can't trigger you any more. When you are pro-active in healing yourself, you will beat any trigger before it can even enter your zone. Acknowledging your triggers is the first step to seeing the mirrors.

***

9

Ask the Right Questions

You can only have the right answers if you ask the right questions. There is an online platform called 'Quora', where people ask questions and those who know the subject or are experts answer. What I have observed is that more than 50 per cent of the questions asked are so vague that no matter how good one knows the subject, it is difficult to answer. If these type of questions are addressed to me, I usually click on the pass option, because I can't figure out what is it that the person is seeking. At other times, there are questions about other people's lives, and I sit there in amusement; how idle a mind must be to ask questions about other people. I am quite sure that is how the universe deals with your confused, meaningless questions and demands. It would say pass!

In case an answer is given, it would match the question. Quora has made me realise why we are a confused lot. We are not being taught how to ask questions. It is only the right questions that would lead to the correct answer or the desired resolution, not just any question. Don't ask useless questions—Why did this happen to me? Why do people behave this way? Why is life so unfair? With due regard to what you may be going through, and how hurt you may be, those are incredibly wrong questions; they bring you only confusion as an answer. Even though the journey for most people starts with 'Why Questions', those are the wrong ones if you wish to move forward. While asking questions, keep in mind two important facts:

Your questions bring you answers to what you are asking and not necessarily the resolution to your challenge.

Know whom are you asking. The answers to your challenges stemming out of your universe will be found within your universe. Hence you need to seek answers from yourself and not try and find out answers in other's lives.

The questions you can ask in any given situation that would bring you meaningful insight can be:

o   What in me is creating this?

o   What is my need to go through this challenge?

o   What is the lesson I have been missing?

o   What is the gift of this challenge?

o   What is it that the universe is trying to tell me?

o   How can I change it?

o   What should I do, or how should I be, for the truth to unfold, for the lesson to be learnt, with total ease?

o   What is it in this situation that I am not seeing? Is this my mirror? Is it a projection? What is this person/situation reflecting back at me?

o   What am I missing here?

o   How can I create another possibility that's easy and fun? What other choices do I have?

o   Do I have a choice to change it? If yes, let the universe show me the way.

o   If I would have had no fear, what would I be doing?

Asking the right question is what changes the answer which would eventually lead you to the correct resolution. Though this is a critical step and the key to the solution or a resolution, it is just 20 per cent of the game. The tricky part is your ability to receive the answer. You need willingness, an open mind, a courageous heart, loads of patience and an always-on-the-toes practice of awareness.

I heard a story once. A man was standing at the door of his friend's home, knocking on the door. The host shouted from inside: Come on in, the door is open. The man kept pressing the door handle down and pushing the door, and yet the door did not open. After a few attempts, frustrated, he shouted: The door is locked, do you mind opening the door? The host replied: You need to pull the handle up and pull the door towards yourself, then the door opens. Don't be that guest. Knock on the door of the universe, show your presence and your desire to resolve, and then drop your knowing. Be open for the answers to show up in ways unexpected. Answers would come, you don't even have to try and find them, but only if you are open and willing to receive.

In all these years of my work, one thing has been very evident: 100 per cent of the times, people with rigidity and a sense of strong judgement either about self or others, recover from their challenges and diseases much slower, and with much more difficulty, than those who are open and willing to know it all and see it all. It takes much more effort to work with rigid people; usually, there are relapses and complications.

I remember the case of a cancer patient. No matter how my heart was feeling the pain of the family, no matter how much I wanted to help, each time I sat in meditation, my guides asked me not to interfere. The case came to me in 2017. We did a couple of sessions, and he recovered maybe 60 per cent, but I knew more work was to be done. Then they shifted to another therapist since I was away for a month, and when I got back, the relapse had happened. We again worked on it from the root level, and again there was 60 per cent improvement, and I gave some instructions to be followed.

When he talked to me last, he said, "Sahar, I can't help it, I cannot forgive from my heart. I do not feel happy when I see others progress. I am very bitter with life, and I cannot change that." After that, I knew I had to stop working with him. As a therapist, I was aware of the distress and agony, but what can anyone do if the soul is unwilling? I did a few more healings till eventually, my 'Guides' told me: 'No more!' You only receive help if you are willing to see and acknowledge and make efforts to change.

In another case, a beautiful young lady attended my 'Law of Attraction' workshop a few years ago. She messaged me two months later, sending me a note of 'Gratitude.' She said she was working and she had found her ideal job. After two years, she attended a 'Family Constellation', and later she told me that within six months of the constellation, she got married. She had mentioned in her message her parents had been looking for a match for her for the past few years. She attended another constellation and moved to London with her husband a couple of months later. When someone is open and willing, the universe forces its way through to give all that which is blissful for the seeker. When I say be in allowance, I am asking you to be completely ready to see as well as know all that has been in regards with yourself and everyone involved in the situation you are currently in. Just remind yourself, you have been travelling for eternity, and you would continue to travel for eternity. You, like anyone else, have been there, done that.

You have done it, so how would seeing it make you any better or worse?

***

10

Give Benefit of the Doubt

Always and in every situation, give yourself and all others benefit of the doubt. Not because someone is right or wrong, but because you would be doing yourself a huge favour. When you practice this simple habit, you save yourself from a lot of future 'karma.' You may even save a relationship and meanwhile, you get time to reflect and respond instead of reacting.

Everything eventually boils down to you and your choices. No matter who is doing what and no matter how certain people have behaved and made you feel, the fact is that you chose those experiences and those very people to do exactly what you asked them to do. Have more gratitude for people with a negative role in your life; they agreed to play the villain. Anyone can be the hero; it takes courage to be the bad guy.

The other primary need of human beings after survival is that of honour. If I ask you today to play a game in which for forty-eight hours I announce everywhere that you stole my wallet or killed my dog or anything to defame you, you would not agree to play it even as a game, or as a prank pulled on others. How strong and helpful are those souls who agree to play the bad guy for lifetimes, so that you can learn? Don't you think they deserve a salute? Remember, there is always a positive and a negative perspective of everything. What and how you choose to look at things determines the direction and the challenges of the way. You are the Creator of every moment of your life and can make better choices. You can change your life, its direction and the way life is happening. You are the one who decides whether life is happening for you or against you. These simple points can change your life only if you apply them regularly. If you are diligent, you would one day see your truth, your light, your power and your might.

***

11

Forgive Yourself

Learn to accept and approve of yourself, so that you can love yourself. Forgiving others is a lot easier than forgiving ourselves. People with mental conditions such as schizophrenia, depression, Alzheimer's, drug addictions, et al. are the ones who are escaping their own selves. We can be extremely angry with our own selves for the choices we have made that we prefer to forget them. Or maybe we are so ashamed of our life story that we rather live many different lives or keep leaving this reality and escape our truth. It is important to forgive yourself. Remind yourself that whatever has happened is because you had to experience a certain aspect of this existence. It will help you judge yourself less. Let me remind you, whatever happened in your life occurred with the Source's consent, it happened because it was allowed and because the divine so wished. If the Source can forgive you and give you chances, why can't you forgive yourself?

Remind yourself that everything is always for your highest good even if it is causing you shame, guilt and regret at this moment. See the brilliance of your life.

Stop taking yourself seriously. Life is supposed to be fun;

after all, other than our breath, we own nothing. We played a role in the 'Universal Studio' where billions of movies are being shot every day, and we would have a better role if we learn the art of 'conscious roleplay.'

You are responsible only for yourself. Your only responsibility is to live your life fully and consciously with only one objective: 'To evolve with ease, joy and grace.' There is absolutely no need for suffering. 'Suffering' is the programming of your ego; 'Ease', however, is the language of your soul. Choose the soul always; it knows how to have fun.

Focus on 'being' and not 'doing.' When you allow yourself to be, you allow life to flow through you. It is like the universe is your chauffeur—it will take you wherever you need to go while you sit back and enjoy the ride.

If you take nothing else from this book, I want you to know and believe, you are as beautiful and as special as anyone else. This truth is only and only for you to unearth and believe. It is not important if others know your truth. It is not necessary to know it all; it is not important to do it all and have it all. What is important is to have the desire for things to show up—for wounds to heal, for challenges to resolve, for progress to take place, for changes to happen, for joy to take over. You may feel lost and not know where to head, but if you are stubborn enough to hold on to the path, in the end, all will make sense. Till then, even if you know nothing else, be grateful and forgiving. And when you don't know how, 'Fake It Till You Faith It.'

***

12

The False Alarm of Separation

In this book, I've spoken about how almost every soul fears separation and is convinced that its separation from the Source is a clear rejection by it. It has been quite interesting to witness this belief existing within every single soul I have come across and the consequences of it. The belief of separation is the root cause of all evil within man's mind. It causes a lack of selfworth and self-love; a feeling of inadequacy, jealousy and depression, et al.

On March 14th 2020, I was guided to do some healing for the infamous Covid-19 virus, which had been declared as a pandemic.

Though I cannot share the details of what a group of students and I witnessed, I do wish to share with you, my readers, the profound and life-changing message that followed after the healing.

The message unfolded as follows:

Life is created, and it thrives when the cells multiply and separate from each other. It's only in separation that life can be co-created. If you watch nature closely, you see it is through separation that life expands. Look at human beings, for example. Sperms are produced in millions in a man's body. They are then separated from their source (his body) and made to enter another space. Similarly, there are many eggs in the woman's body, but only one egg and one sperm, separated from their source, get together to create another life. The new cell keeps getting divided, yet it remains united for a new life to start and grow.

You, humans, have got it all wrong. You don't know how, what, and when to divide. You don't know when and how to unite; hence you're destroying the planet—dispelling life.

Your fundamental perception of life has been twisted. You need to see the whole of humanity as one body. One part gets wounded and bleeds, one organ fails, so eventually, the whole system would collapse. But you don't get it. Covid-19, even though human-made, created by those who think cutting their body part would help them win the race, is a divine plan. It is a conspiracy to reset human consciousness back to its original factory setting which is of love and oneness.

To teach you that you are only separated by your beauty and uniqueness, divided by your special abilities and skills so that in time of need, you can hold the space and help each other. To be able to stand by each other and have each other's back. Like different parts of a machine that are supposed to work together to allow the end product to be ready—your evolution. It is to unite you in relearning how to maintain life and facilitate evolution.

Separation creates life, but unity is what maintains life.

As we separate at the end of this book, I'm sure we will unite again to hold life and facilitate evolution yet again. Perhaps, we shall meet in the 'Book of Secrets.' And soon.

Au revoir!

***

ALSO BY THE SAME AUTHOR

Stories From the Past Life

Because
Time
Does Not
Heal

Sahar Gharachorlou

Because Time Does Not Heal
ISBN: 978-93-92210-10-5

Delving deep into Past Life Regression, therapist and coach Sahar Gharachorlou travels into ten people's past lives, helping them see through their challenges and recover from memories of trauma carried across lifetimes.

If you have feelings of déjà vu, if you wonder why your relationships are a mess, if places or persons make you feel eerie, then this book holds the answers. With her gentle words and insurmountable patience, Sahar addresses the ordinary person's anxieties, insecurities and illnesses. Her case studies provide readers with clarity as she wipes away layers of our muddy lives.

Because Time Does Not Heal draws from our lived experience and illuminates the path to healing body and soul.